The
Baseball
Geek's Bible

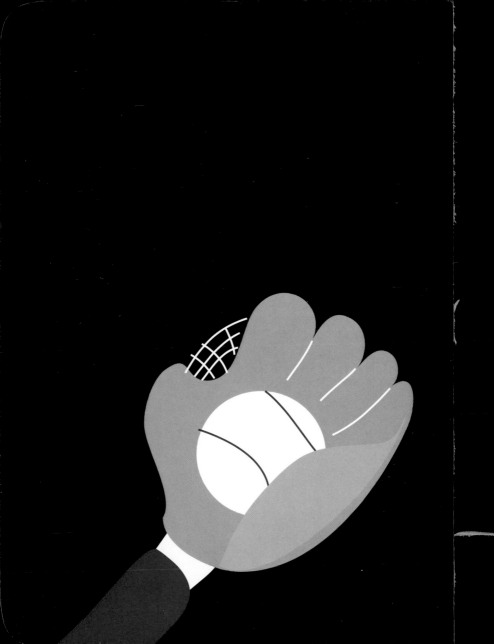

The Baseball Geek's Bible

Douglas B. Lyons

MQ Publications Ltd

Published by MQ Publications Ltd
12 The Ivories
6–8 Northampton Street
London N1 2HY
Tel: 020 7359 2244
Fax: 020 7359 1616
Email: mail@mqpublications.com

North American office
49 West 24th Street
New York, NY 10010
Email: information@mqpublicationsus.com

Website: www.mqpublications.com

ISBN: 1-84072-800-0

1 3 5 7 9 0 8 6 4 2

Printed in China

Contents

Introduction

More than any other sport, baseball is a game of moments. Game-winning home runs, game-ending triple plays, steals of home, milestone strikeouts, infamous errors, beanings, impossible catches, ejections, Eddie Gaedel, and the Miracle Mets. One of the things I love about the game is that many of baseball's most memorable moments are not connected with who won and who lost, or who hit a home run.

These are my picks for the most memorable moments involving major league ballgames, players, events, and transactions since 1900. Some of your favorites may be here. Some are not. They'll be in your book.

To save time, space, and repetitive explanations, I have referred to teams by their current commonly used names. So you won't find references to the Naps (Cleveland Indians), the Highlanders (New York Yankees), the Pilgrims (Boston Red Sox), etc.

If your favorite baseball moment is not here, let me know. Perhaps I'll include it in the next edition of this book. Email me at BASBALINFO@AOL.COM.

I would like to thank Jeffrey Lyons. My older brother by three years, Jeffrey is the coauthor, with me (so far) of *Out of Left Field*, *Curveballs and Screwballs*, and *Short Hops and Foul Tips*. He has been a baseball fan/Boston Red Sox fan—the two are indistinguishable for him—since birth and has forgotten more about the game and its history than most people know. (Jeff is the one who actually bought one of those signs which says PARKING FOR RED SOX FANS ONLY!) If it were not for Jeff, I would not be a baseball fan or a baseball writer.

Thanks also to Fred Bennett, Maxwell Kates, David Vincent, and Tim Wiles, Director of Research at the Baseball Hall of Fame in Cooperstown for his consistent enthusiastic help and support.

This book would not have been possible without the incredible material available on line at www.retrosheet.org.

I also want to acknowledge the Society for American Baseball Research (SABR): www.sabr.org. If you love baseball, you'll love SABR. I love both.

May all your days be baseball days!

Firsts
& lasts

*"If a horse can't eat it,
I don't want to play on it."*

Dick Allen, about artificial turf

THE AMERICAN WAY

The American League is organized in Milwaukee on January 28, 1901. Team rosters are limited to 14 players.

STARS IN STRIPES

The home uniforms of the New York Yankees feature pinstripes for the first time on April 11, 1912.

Going out in style

Christy Mathewson of the Reds and Mordecai "Three Finger" Brown of the Cubs face each other on the mound by special arrangement on September 4, 1916. The game is the last for both. Each goes the distance. Mathewson wins 10–8. The win is Mathewson's 373rd, and his only game not in a New York Giants uniform.

NOW HEAR THIS!

THE PIRATES–PHILLIES GAME AT FORBES FIELD ON AUGUST 5, 1921, IS THE FIRST MAJOR LEAGUE GAME BROADCAST ON RADIO, BY HAROLD ARLIN ON KDKA IN PITTSBURGH.

WELCOME TO THE CLUB

Ken Williams of the St. Louis Browns becomes the first member of the 30/30 club—in 1922, with 30 home runs and 30 stolen bases in the same season. Williams finishes with 39 home runs and 37 steals.

The Georgia Peach's last hit

Ty Cobb of the Philadelphia As gets the last hit of his career—#4,189—on September 3, 1928. It's a pinch-hit double off Bump Hadley of the Senators.

NOW BATTING, #1
Earle Combs is the first Yankee to bat wearing a uniform number (#1) on Opening Day, April 18, 1929.

WORKING OVERTIME

The first man to hit a pinch-hit grand slam in extra innings is Rogers Hornsby of the Cubs in the 11th inning on September 13, 1931.

FIRST MIDSUMMER CLASSIC

The first All-Star Game is held in Chicago's Comiskey Park on July 6, 1933, with the American League defeating the National League 4–2 as Babe Ruth homers twice.

LET THERE BE LIGHT!

President Franklin D. Roosevelt throws a switch at the White House on May 24, 1935 and the lights go on at Crosley Field in Cincinnati for the first major league night game. The Reds defeat the Phillies 2–1.

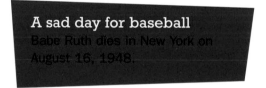

A sad day for baseball

Babe Ruth dies in New York on August 16, 1948.

SEEING THE LIGHT

The Philadelphia Athletics host the Cleveland Indians at Shibe Park on May 16, 1939, and lose 8–3 in the first night game in the American League.

BUT STILL NO INSTANT REPLAY

Billy Werber of the Cincinnati Reds becomes the first major leaguer to bat on television on August 26, 1939, as the Reds play the Brooklyn Dodgers at Ebbets Field. Red Barber does the broadcast.

IN A PINCH

Player-manager Joe Cronin of the Boston Red Sox hits pinch-hit home runs in both games of a doubleheader on June 17, 1943, the first man to do so.

Breaking the barrier

American history is made as Jackie Robinson becomes the first modern black player in the major leagues as he takes the field for the Brooklyn Dodgers on April 15, 1947.

LARRY DOBY'S DEBUT

Larry Doby, playing for the Cleveland Indians on July 5, 1947, becomes the first black man to play in the American League.

LAST OF HIS KIND

Jim Hegan of the Indians becomes the last "courtesy runner" in major league baseball. When Ray Boone is hit in the arm with a pitch in the bottom of the 9th inning, Hegan, the Cleveland catcher, runs for Boone and scores, on July 2, 1949.

AN HISTORIC MATCHUP

Pitcher Don Newcombe of the Brooklyn Dodgers faces Hank Thompson of the New York Giants—the first time a black pitcher faces a black batter, July 8, 1949.

A TRUE ALL-STAR GAME

BLACK PLAYERS APPEAR IN THE ALL-STAR GAME FOR THE FIRST TIME ON JULY 12, 1949, WHEN ROY CAMPANELLA, JACKIE ROBINSON, DON NEWCOMBE, AND LARRY DOBY TAKE THE FIELD IN BROOKLYN.

OPENING DAY = OPENING NIGHT

For the first time, a team's first game of the season is played at night as the Cardinals beat the Pirates 4–2 in St. Louis, April 18, 1950.

ALL BASES COVERED

Opening Day, April 15, 1952 is the first day in which all games feature four umpires, which becomes the standard.

SO LONG, ST. LOUIS

The St. Louis Browns play their final game on September 27, 1953, losing at home 2–1 to the Chicago White Sox. They move to Baltimore in 1954 to become the Orioles.

HELLO BALTIMORE

Reviving a name that had been a city tradition for generations, the American League Baltimore Orioles, formerly the St. Louis Browns, play their first game on April 13, 1954, a 3–0 loss in Detroit.

"Hammering" Hank breaks in

Hank Aaron's first major league game for the Milwaukee Braves takes place on April 13, 1954, Opening Day in Cincinnati. It is also the first game in which outfielders bring their gloves in between innings instead of leaving them on the field.

WATCH WHAT YOU'RE DOING!

In a game between the Yankees and the Senators in Washington on April 18, 1956, Ed Rommel of the American League becomes the first major league umpire to wear glasses during a game.

CALIFORNIA, HERE WE COME

The Brooklyn Dodgers play their final game, losing 2–1 to the Philadelphia Phillies at Philadelphia on September 29, 1957. Before the 1958 season, the Dodgers move to Los Angeles.

California, here we come (2)

The New York Giants play their last game in the Polo Grounds before moving to San Francisco for the 1958 season on September 29, 1957, Pirates 9, Giants 1.

WHAT TOOK THEM SO LONG?

Elijah "Pumpsie" Green makes his debut with the Boston Red Sox—the last team to integrate—on July 21, 1959, 12 years after Jackie Robinson broke the color line with the Brooklyn Dodgers.

TWO FOR THE MONEY

In an effort to raise money for the players' pension fund, two All-Star Games are played in the same year. The American League wins the second one 5–3 on August 3, 1959 after the National League won 5–4 at Pittsburgh on July 7. Two All-Star Games were played each season from 1959 to 1963.

WHO IS THAT?

THANKS TO OWNER BILL VEECK, THE CHICAGO WHITE SOX BECOME THE FIRST TEAM TO HAVE PLAYERS' NAMES ON THEIR BACKS IN 1960.

And now for something completely different

On April 11, 1961, the Chicago Cubs open the season as no other team ever has: with no manager. Cubs' owner P.K. Wrigley decides to use a "College of Coaches" instead of one manager. Vedie Himsl, Harry Craft, El Tappe, and Lou Klein do a dreadful job, finishing the season with a record of 64–90.

MEET THE METS

The New York Mets play their first game on April 11, 1962. Their third baseman is Don Zimmer. The Mets lose 11–4 to the St. Louis Cardinals, a portent of things to come. The Mets lose 119 more games during the season, winning just 40 games in 1962.

THANK YOU, MR. PRESIDENT

John F. Kennedy throws out the first pitch of the first All-Star Game at D.C. Stadium in Washington on July 10, 1962, the first president to do so. The National Leaguers win 3–1.

Polo Grounds farewell

The New York Mets, the third major league team to call the Polo Grounds home, play the last game there on September 17, 1963, losing to the Phillies 5–1. On April 17, 1964, they move into their new home, Shea Stadium.

THE GREAT INDOORS

The first major league game is played indoors on April 12, 1965, at Houston's Astrodome, home of the Astros. The Pittsburgh Pirates beat them 2–0.

YOU DON'T HAVE TO MOW IT, EITHER

The first game on artificial turf is played on April 8, 1966 at the Astrodome as the Astros host the Los Angeles Dodgers. The ersatz grass is dubbed "Astroturf."

ANOTHER BARRIER FALLS
EMMETT ASHFORD BECOMES THE FIRST BLACK MAN
TO UMPIRE IN A MAJOR LEAGUE GAME ON OCTOBER
11, 1966 AS THE CLEVELAND INDIANS BEAT THE
SENATORS 5–2 AT WASHINGTON.

ONE OF A KIND
Frank Robinson of the Baltimore Orioles becomes the
first (and still the only) man to be named Most
Valuable Player in both leagues when he is voted the
MVP of the American League on November 8, 1966.
He was the MVP of the National League in 1961
when he was with the Reds.

INDOOR ALL-STARS
The All-Star Game is played indoors for the first
time, at the Astrodome in Houston on July 9, 1968.
The National League squeaked out a 1–0 victory.

A CANADIAN FIRST
The Expos host the first major league game played
outside the United States on April 14, 1969 as they
beat the St. Louis Cardinals 8–7 at Montreal's
Jarry Park.

THE LAST PILOT PITCHER
MIGUEL FUENTES IS SHOT AND KILLED IN A BAR FIGHT IN PUERTO RICO ON JANUARY 29, 1970. HE PITCHED THE FINAL INNING FOR THE SEATTLE PILOTS BEFORE A "CROWD" OF 5,473 ON OCTOBER 2, 1969. THE PILOTS MOVED TO MILWAUKEE THE FOLLOWING SEASON, BECOMING THE BREWERS.

A PAIR OF HISTORIC BLASTERS
For the first time ever, on June 17, 1970, home runs are hit in the same game by two men who have over 500 home runs: Willie Mays (Giants, 615) and Ernie Banks (Cubs, 504) in San Francisco.

YOU'RE ON THE AIR
Former National Leaguer slugger Bill White becomes a Yankee broadcaster on February 10, 1971—the first black announcer in the game.

FIRST ALL-MINORITY LINEUP
Pittsburgh manager Danny Murtaugh makes history on September 1, 1971 when he writes out the Pirates' lineup for the game. All he's trying to do is win the pennant. But the names he writes out constitute the first all-minority lineup:
Rennie Stennett, second base
Gene Clines, center field
Roberto Clemente, right field
Willie Stargell, left field
Manny Sanguillen, catcher

Dave Cash, third base
Al Oliver, first base
Jackie Hernandez, shortstop
Dock Ellis, pitcher

The Pirates win the ballgame 10–7 over the Phillies and go on to win the World Series a month later.

A wild farewell

The Senators are beating the Yankees 7–5 with two outs in the top of the ninth inning, in their final home game on September 30, 1971 before their 1972 move to Texas to become the Rangers. But fans jump on and start tearing up the field looking for souvenirs. When they cannot clear the field, the umpires forfeit the game to the Yankees.

WILLIE MAYS' FINAL HOME RUN

Willie Mays of the New York Mets hits his 660th and final home run on August 17, 1973 off Don Gullett of the Reds.

MOVE OVER, SANDY

On September 27, 1973, the last day of the season, Nolan Ryan of the Angels strikes out the last Twins batter of the game, Rich Reese, Ryan's 16th strikeout of the game and 383rd of the season —to break Sandy Koufax's single-season record.

JACKIE WOULD HAVE BEEN PROUD
FRANK ROBINSON MANAGES THE CLEVELAND INDIANS ON APRIL 8, 1975—THE FIRST BLACK MAN TO MANAGE A MAJOR LEAGUE TEAM. ROBINSON, THE TRIBE'S PLAYER-MANAGER ALSO HOMERS AS THEY BEAT THE YANKEES 5-3.

Hammerin' Hank bows out
Hank Aaron plays his final game—#3,298—on October 3, 1976. He singles in the 6th inning and is lifted for pinch runner Jim Gantner. Had Aaron stayed in the game and scored (as Gantner did), Aaron would have broken his tie with Babe Ruth at the #2 spot (now #3) for most runs scored in a career—2,174.

A SEATTLE ORIGINAL
Pitcher Diego Segui is the only man in history to play in the very first game for two teams in the same league in the same city. Segui is in the first game of the Seattle Pilots on April 8, 1969. On April 6, 1977 he plays in the first game for the Seattle Mariners.

QS ALL AROUND!

THE FIRST ALL-"Q" BATTERY TAKES THE FIELD ON APRIL 13, 1980 AS RELIEVER DAN QUISENBERRY OF THE KANSAS CITY ROYALS PITCHES TO CATCHER JAMIE QUIRK.

SAVE ME

Rollie Fingers becomes the first pitcher to save 300 games, as his Brewers beat the Seattle Mariners on April 21, 1982.

Play ball, eh?

The first All-Star Game outside the United States is played at Olympic Stadium in Montreal, Quebec, Canada on July 13, 1982. The National League wins 4–1.

NEVER HAPPENED BEFORE AND PROBABLY NEVER WILL AGAIN

Joel Youngblood becomes the first man to get hits for different teams in different cities on the same day, August 4, 1982.

First, he drives in a run for the Mets as New York beats the Cubs. After his trade to Montreal, he flies to Philadelphia and singles for the Expos against the Phillies.

Going, going, gone

On the 50th anniversary of the first All-Star
Game, Fred Lynn hits the first grand slam in
All-Star Game history, July 6, 1983 at
Chicago's Comiskey Park, the site of that
first midsummer classic.

NEVER HAPPENED BEFORE DEPT.
Dwight Evans, leading off for the Boston Red
Sox on Opening Day, April 7, 1986, does
something which no player has ever done:
he hits a home run on the first pitch of the
season in Detroit off Jack Morris of the Tigers.

TAKE A SEAT, PETE

Goose Gossage of the San Diego Padres strikes out
Pete Rose of the Cincinnati Reds on August 17,
1986—Rose's last at-bat.

IN THE CITY OF BROTHERLY LOVE
Rookie brothers start against each other on
the mound for the first time on September 29,
1986, at the Vet in Philadelphia as Greg
Maddux of the Cubs beats his older brother
Mike of the Phillies, 6–3.

THOSE ARE MY BOYS!

Cal Ripken, Sr. is the first man to manage two sons on the same team in the majors on July 11, 1987, when Billy Ripken joins his brother Cal, Jr. on the Baltimore Orioles.

LIGHTS ON AT WRIGLEY

Wrigley Field in Chicago, home of the Cubs, is the last stadium to install lights and the last team to play a night game at home. The Cubs start their first night game at home on August 8, 1988 against the Philadelphia Phillies The game is rained out after 3 innings, however. The skies clear up the next night, and the Cubs beat the New York Mets 6–4.

ANOTHER FIRST

On February 2, 1989 Bill White, former major leaguer and Yankee broadcaster, is elected president of the National League—the first black man to hold such a high post in professional sports in the United States.

WHAT A MISERABLE DAY FOR A BALLGAME. LET'S PLAY TWO!

On June 5, 1989, the first game is played at the first major league stadium with a retractable roof. The team? The Toronto Blue Jays. The stadium? "Skydome." (Now called "Rogers Centre.") The Milwaukee Brewers win 5–3.

IS IT INDOORS OR OUTDOORS? BOTH!

The Blue Jays–Brewers game in Toronto on June 7, 1989, is played indoors. The Blue Jays–Brewers game in Toronto on June 7, 1989, is played outdoors. Stop! You're both right! When the game starts, Skydome's roof is open and the game is outdoors. But threatening weather in the fifth inning leads to the roof being closed. The game continues indoors—the first game played both indoors and outdoors, with the Blue Jays winning 4–2.

BANG! BANG! ZOOM! ZOOM!

Ken Griffey, Sr. and Jr. become the first father and son to homer for the same team in the same game on September 14, 1990. They homer in the top of the first inning for the Seattle Mariners as they lose to the California Angels 7–5. Kirk McCaskill becomes the first pitcher to give up home runs to a father and son in the same inning (the seventh) and in the same game.

LIKE FATHER, LIKE SON

KEN GRIFFEY, SR. AND JR. BECOME THE FIRST FATHER AND SON PAIR TO BE NAMED MOST VALUABLE PLAYERS IN THE ALL-STAR GAME WHEN JUNIOR WINS THE AWARD ON JULY 14, 1992. SENIOR WON THE AWARD IN 1980.

Farewell to Comiskey

The final game at the first Comiskey Park is played on September 30, 1990. The White Sox edge the Mariners 2–1. In 1991, the team moves into its new Chicago home, also called Comiskey Park, later named "U.S. Cellular Field."

LIKE GRANDFATHER, LIKE FATHER, LIKE SON

Bret Boone makes his major league debut on August 19, 1992 at second base for the Mariners in a game against Baltimore. He is the first major leaguer whose father (Bob) and grandfather (Ray) also played in the majors.

PLAY BALL, MR. PRESIDENT

Bill Clinton becomes the first president to throw out a ceremonial first pitch on Opening Day from the pitcher's mound at Baltimore's Camden Yards on April 4, 1993.

BANG ZOOM! BANG ZOOM!

Carlos Baerga of the Cleveland Indians does something which no player has ever done before—on April 8, 1993, he hits home runs from both sides of the plate in the same inning.

PLAY BALL, MATE!

Pitcher Graeme Lloyd and catcher Dave Nilsson of the Milwaukee Brewers become the first all-Australian battery in the majors on April 11, 1993.

OLÉ!

For the first time, a major league baseball game is played in a country other than the United States and Canada. On August 16, 1996, in Monterrey, Mexico, the San Diego Padres beat the New York Mets 15–10.

30-30 VISION

Barry Larkin of the Cincinnati Reds becomes the first shortstop with 30 homers and 30 stolen bases in a season on September 22, 1996.

ANOTHER CANADIAN FIRST

Larry Walker of the Colorado Rockies in the National League, a native of Maple Ridge, British Columbia, is the first Canadian to be named Most Valuable Player (1997).

WOW! THE GIANTS PLAY THE RANGERS! WOW!

For the first time in the modern history of baseball, teams from different leagues play each other in regular season games on June 12, 1997 at the start of regularly scheduled interleague play. The San Francisco Giants of the National League beat the Texas Rangers of the American League in Texas 4–3.

WINDY CITY SHOWDOWN

The Chicago White Sox play the Chicago Cubs for the first time in regular season play on June 16, 1997 at Comiskey Park. The Cubs win 8–3.

> *PLAY BALL!*
> *For the first time in history, the baseball season opens in a country not called "The United States" or "Canada." The Rockies beat the Padres at Estadio de Beisbol in Monterrey, Mexico on April 4, 1999.*

TOUCH 'EM ALL. TWICE.

Fernando Tatis of the St. Louis Cardinals does something on April 23, 1999, which had never been done before: he hits two grand slams in the same inning—the third. They were the first grand slams of his career. Tatis sets another record—eight RBIs in one inning. Chan Ho Park of the Dodgers gives up both grand slams in that inning to the same batter—the first pitcher ever to do that.

Talk about an away game!

For the first time in history, major league baseball comes to Puerto Rico. The Toronto Blue Jays beat the Texas Rangers 8–1 on Opening Day at Hiram Bithorn Stadium on April 1, 2001.

WHAT A WAY TO SAY FAREWELL

Cal Ripken, Jr., an All-Star for the 19th time, comes to bat in the All-Star Game for the final time in the third inning on July 9, 2001, at Safeco Field in Seattle. He goes out with a bang, hitting a home run off Chan Ho Park on the first pitch. He is named the MVP of the game, 10 years after winning the award in 1991.

A DOMINICAN FIRST

Dominican managers oppose each other for the first time on June 25, 2002, as Luis Pujols leads his Tigers against the Kansas City Royals, led by Tony Peña. The Royals beat the Tigers 8–6.

I NEVER SAW THAT BEFORE

JOHN VADER WAL HITS A PINCH-HIT GRAND SLAM FOR THE MILWAUKEE BREWERS, AND CRAIG WILSON HITS A PINCH-HIT GRAND SLAM FOR THE PIRATES. THIS GAME, ON JULY 17, 2003, IS THE FIRST WITH TWO PINCH-HIT GRAND SLAMS AS THE BREWERS TOP THE PIRATES 7–5.

MAN OF STEAL

On August 29, 2003, batting second for the first time in his 3,076th game, Rickey Henderson steals second base in the third inning—his record 1,406th and final stolen base in the majors, unless he makes another comeback.

I'M NUMBER ONE! I'M NUMBER ONE!

When David Aardsma of the Giants makes his debut on April 6, 2004, he bumps Hank Aaron from his #1 spot alphabetically in the all-time list of major league players.

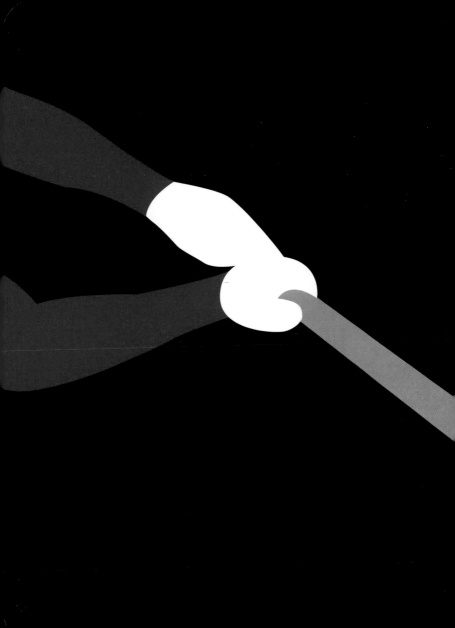

Hitting

*"Hitting a baseball—
it's the hardest thing
to do in sports."*

Ted Williams

MR. 3,000

Honus Wagner of the Pittsburgh Pirates gets his 3,000th hit—the first man to do so in the 20th century, June 9, 1914.

Both sides now

Wally Schang of the Philadelphia As is the first person to hit homers from both sides of the plate in the same game, on September 8, 1916.

JUST PEACHY

TY COBB, OF THE DETROIT TIGERS, THE "GEORGIA PEACH," GETS HIS 3,000TH HIT ON AUGUST 19, 1921.

SUNNY DAY

On September 16, 1924, "Sunny" Jim Bottomley of the St. Louis Cardinals, a future Hall of Famer, drives in 12 runs in one game as St. Louis pounds Brooklyn 17–3.

Totally great

Ty Cobb of the Detroit Tigers homers three times, has a double and two singles—racking up 16 total bases—on May 5, 1925.

NEW MEANING FOR THE PHRASE "2 AND 2"

Future Hall of Famer Max Carey becomes the first player to collect two hits in an inning twice in one game on June 22, 1925: two singles in the first and two more in the eighth inning, helping the Pirates rout the Cardinals 24–6.

HEY YOU KIDS, DON'T TRY THIS AT HOME
Future Hall of Fame pitcher Burleigh Grimes of the Brooklyn Dodgers has about as bad a day as you can have on a baseball field on September 22, 1925. He manages to hit into two double plays and a triple play—three swings, seven outs.

MR. 4,000

Ty Cobb of the Philadelphia Athletics gets his 4,000th hit on July 18, 1927. He is one of only two players to reach that figure, Pete Rose joining him 57 years later.

A RUTHIAN MILESTONE

Babe Ruth of the New York Yankees hits his 500th home run on August 11, 1929.

A driving force

Hack Wilson of the Cubs drives in his 191st run of the season on September 28, 1930—a record which still stands, 75 plus years later.

IRON HORSE-POWER

Lou Gehrig hits four home runs in one game in Philadelphia on June 3, 1932—the first man to do so.

700 CLUB

Babe Ruth hits career home run #700 on July 13, 1934.

SIMPLY GRAND

Tony "Poosh 'Em Up!" Lazzeri of the Yankees becomes the first man to hit two grand slams in one game on May 24, 1936.

FOUR IN ONE

Chuck Klein of the Philadelphia Phillies hits four home runs in a game on July 10, 1936.

A home run with a name

Gabby Hartnett of the Cubs homers off Mace Brown at dusk at Wrigley Field (which did not have lights) on September 28, 1938, to help the Cubs beat the Pirates, and win the National League pennant. The homer becomes known as "The Homer in the Gloamin'."

ONE OF EACH

Johnny Lucadello of the Browns homers from both sides of the plate on September 16, 1940—his only homers of the season.

DOUBLE XX CONNECTS

Jimmie Foxx of the Boston Red Sox hits his 500th career home run on September 24, 1940.

THE THUMPER SAVES THE DAY

On July 8, 1941, the All-Star Game is held at Briggs Stadium in Detroit. In the bottom of the ninth inning, Ted Williams of the Red Sox wins the game with a three-run homer—one of the most dramatic in All-Star history.

THE STREAK ENDS

New York Yankee Joe DiMaggio's 56-game hitting streak, which started on May 15, ends on July 17, 1941. Indians pitchers Al Smith and Jim Bagby plus third baseman Ken Keltner's sparkling defense keep DiMaggio hitless.

HOW TO HIT .400

On September 28, the last day of the 1941 season, Ted Williams of the Red Sox is batting .399955. He can sit out both games of a Sox–Athletics doubleheader, and finish the season with a rounded-off batting average of .400. But Williams plays in both games, goes 6-for-8, and raises his season average to .406 (.4057).

THAT'S A LOT OF HOME RUNS
At the Polo Grounds in New York, Mel Ott of the Giants becomes the first National Leaguer to hit his 500th home run on August 1, 1945.

WHAT A WAY TO WIN A BATTING TITLE!

George "Snuffy" Stirnweiss of the New York Yankees goes 3-for-5 in a Yankee victory over the Red Sox. Although he has not led the American League in batting on any other day during the season, he moves into first place on September 30, 1945, batting .3085443, just .000866 ahead of Tony Cuccinello's .3084577. Because it is the last day of the season, Stirnweiss wins the batting title.

BANG! ZOOM! X 4

PAT SEERY OF THE CHICAGO WHITE SOX HITS FOUR HOME RUNS IN ONE GAME ON JULY 18, 1948.

Four round trips

Gil Hodges of the Brooklyn Dodgers hits four
home runs on August 31, 1950.

BANG, BANG!

Bob Neiman of the St. Louis Browns becomes the
first player to homer in his first two at-bats in the
majors on September 14, 1951.

THE GIANTS WIN THE PENNANT!

Because the New York Giants and the Brooklyn
Dodgers finished the season with identical 96–58
records, a three-game playoff decides the pennant
race. Each team wins one game, setting up the third
and deciding game, October 3, 1951.

With the Giants trailing 4–2 in the bottom of the
ninth inning, Bobby Thomson of the Giants homers
with two men on base off Brooklyn reliever Ralph
Branca, who wears uniform #13. Thomson's home run
will be known as the "shot heard 'round the world."

What was future Hall of Famer Dave Winfield doing
that day? He was busy being born in St. Paul,
Minnesota.

ONE AND DONE

Pitcher Hoyt Wilhelm starts off with a bang. In his very first at-bat on April 23, 1952, in his second major league game, he hits a home run for the New York Giants. He then goes homerless for the next 1,068 games—the rest of his 21-year Hall of Fame career.

Three in one

Gene Stephens has three hits and Sammy White scores three times as the Red Sox score 17 runs in the seventh inning against Detroit on June 18, 1953. Boston goes on to defeat Detroit 23–3.

WAY TO GO, JOE!
Joe Adcock of the Milwaukee Braves hits four home runs in a game on July 31, 1954.

LONG BALL

Dale Long of the Pittsburgh Pirates homers in a record eighth consecutive game on May 28, 1956.

ROCKY FOUR

Rocky Colavito of the Cleveland Indians hits four consecutive home runs in a game in Baltimore on June 10, 1959.

A MILESTONE FOR THE KID
Ted Williams hits his 500th career home run, a blast off the Indians' Wynn Hawkins in Cleveland, June 17, 1960.

WHAT A WAY TO GO!
In his final at-bat, Ted Williams of the Red Sox hits career home run #521 in Boston on September 28, 1960.

A-MAYS-ING!
WILLIE MAYS OF THE SAN FRANCISCO GIANTS HITS FOUR HOME RUNS IN A GAME IN MILWAUKEE ON APRIL 30, 1961.

Gentile giant
Jim Gentile of the Orioles hits a grand slam in the first inning and another in the second inning in a 13–5 victory over the Twins on May 9, 1961.

AND FOUR TO GO!
Eddie Mathews, Hank Aaron, Joe Adcock, and Frank Thomas hit back-to-back-to-back-to-back home runs for the Milwaukee Braves on June 8, 1961 and still lose 10–8 to the Reds in Cincinnati.

61 IN '61

On October 1, 1961, Yankee Roger Maris hits his 61st home run of the season off Tracy Stallard of the Boston Red Sox at Yankee Stadium in the final game of the season, breaking the record of 60 set by Babe Ruth in 1927.

CAN'T BUY A HIT

Pitcher Bob Buhl goes 0-for-1962. He came to bat 70 times with the Cubs and the Braves without a hit.

ONE DOWN, 4,255 TO GO

Pete Rose of the Reds gets his first major league hit—a triple off Bob Friend of the Pirates in Cincinnati on April 13, 1963.

ARE YOU COMING OR GOING?

Upon hitting his 100th career home run on June 23, 1963—the only National League homer of his career —Jimmy Piersall of the New York Mets runs around the bases facing backwards. Baseball rules are later changed to prohibit the stunt.

A NICE EVEN NUMBER
Stan Musial of the St. Louis Cardinals gets the final hit (#3,630) of his career on September 29, 1963, a single off Jim Maloney of the Cincinnati Reds, and retires with an even record: 1,815 hits at home, 1,815 hits on the road.

HANK AARON'S 756TH HOME RUN
Hank Aaron of the Braves homers off Curt Simmons of the St. Louis Cardinals on August 18, 1955. But Cardinals catcher Bob Uecker claimed that Aaron was out of the batter's box when he hit the ball. Home plate umpire Chris Pelekoudas agrees. No home run. Aaron is out.

A GIANT STEP
Willie Mays of the San Francisco Giants hits his 500th career home run on September 13, 1965.

ONE PITCHER, TWO GRAND SLAMS
Tony Cloninger, a pitcher for the Atlanta Braves, smacks grand slams in the first and the fourth innings on July 3, 1966 as the Braves beat the Giants in San Francisco 17–3. Cloninger finishes the day with nine RBIs.

A MANTLE MILESTONE
YANKEE MICKEY MANTLE HITS THE 500TH HOME RUN OF HIS CAREER ON MAY 14, 1967.

ASTRO-NOMICAL

In San Francisco, Eddie Mathews of the Houston Astros hits the 500th home run of his career on July 14, 1967. The pitcher is another future Hall of Famer, Juan Marichal of the Giants.

Can I have that one back please?

Brooks Robinson sets a record he wishes he did not hold on August 6, 1967: he hits into the fourth triple play of his career.

AARON'S MILESTONE

IN ATLANTA, HANK AARON HITS THE 500TH HOME RUN OF HIS CAREER, A THREE-RUN HOMER ON JULY 14, 1968.

ROSE BUNTS FOR A BATTING CROWN

Pete Rose wins the batting title on September 29, 1968 by bunting for a single—off Ray Sadecki of the Giants. Rose's batting average is .335.

MAYS DOES IT AGAIN

It's home run #600 for Willie Mays of the Giants on September 22, 1969.

TAKE IT TO THE BANKS

Ernie Banks, "Mr. Cub," hits the 500th home run of his career on May 12, 1970, a second-inning blast off Pat Jarvis of the Braves. One of the umpires is Frank Secory, who also worked the Cubs' game on September 20, 1953, when Banks hit his first home run.

SLAMMIN'

Frank Robinson of the Baltimore Orioles hits a grand slam in the fifth inning against the Washington Senators and another in the sixth on June 26, 1970.

HAMMERED

HANK AARON HITS HIS 600TH HOME RUN ON APRIL 27, 1971.

A BIG ONE FOR THE KILLER

Harmon Killebrew hits the 500th home run of his career on August 10, 1971 at Metropolitan Stadium in Minneapolis.

HERE'S TO YOU, MR. ROBINSON

Frank Robinson of the Baltimore Orioles hits his 500th home run, a ninth inning three-run blast on September 13, 1971.

NATE THE GREAT

On August 1, 1972, Nate Colbert of the San Diego Padres hits five home runs in a doubleheader (two in the first, three in the second), matching a feat performed by Stan Musial on May 2, 1954—a feat the eight-year-old Colbert witnessed as a fan in the stands in St. Louis.

POWER OUTAGE

Rod Carew of the Minnesota Twins wins the 1972 American League batting title with a .318 average, and 0 home runs.

The first tenth man

Ron Blomberg of the New York Yankees becomes the first "Designated Hitter"—batting but not fielding—on April 5, 1973. His bat is on display at the Hall of Fame. But he didn't use it—Blomberg walked.

YOU'RE GETTING TO BE A HABIT WITH ME

Willie McCovey of the San Francisco Giants hits two home runs in an inning for the second time in his career on June 27, 1977. He did it for the first time on April 12, 1973.

OH HENRY!

Hank Aaron of the Atlanta Braves hits career home run #700 on July 21, 1973.

MARTY PEREZ PINCH HITS FOR HANK AARON!

In the fourth inning of a game against the Giants on September 10, 1973, Marty Perez pinch hits for Hank Aaron of the Atlanta Braves. Aaron had homered earlier in the game and his back hurt. Perez grounded out in his first at-bat, then stayed in the game and doubled.

AARON TIES RUTH

In the first inning on April 4, 1974, on Opening Day in Cincinnati, Hank Aaron of the Braves blasts his 714th home run on his first swing of the season, tying Babe Ruth's career record.

AARON PASSES RUTH

In the Braves' home opener at Atlanta's Fulton County Stadium, on April 8, 1974, Hank Aaron hits career home run #715—breaking Babe Ruth's career record which had stood since 1935.

◆- -

HOMETOWN HERO

Al Kaline of the Detroit Tigers gets the 3,000th hit of his career in his hometown of Baltimore, on September 24, 1974.

7-FOR-7

Rennie Stennett of the Pittsburgh Pirates sets a modern record on September 16, 1975 by going 7-for-7 in a nine-inning game as the Pirates annihilate the Cubs 22–0.

Cub killer

Mike Schmidt of the Phillies hits four home runs in one game against the Cubs in Chicago on April 17, 1976—the first National Leaguer to do so in consecutive at-bats.

YANKEE DOODLE DANDY

Chris Chambliss of the New York Yankees bats in the bottom of the ninth inning of the deciding Game 5 of the American League Championship Series on October 14, 1976 at Yankee Stadium. The game is tied at 6. Facing Mark Littell of the Kansas City Royals, Chambliss sends the Yankees to the World Series for the first time in twelve years with a walk-off home run to right field—one of the most dramatic ever. Pandemonium erupts as fans swarm all over the infield. Chambliss circles the bases but can't touch home plate because he can't find it in the sea of humanity. Later, he emerges from the dugout with a police escort to step on the plate.

THAT'S A WRAP!

Hank Aaron of the Milwaukee Brewers breaks his own record for the final time and hits home run #755, the last of his career, July 20, 1976.

Who wants to slide in shorts?

The Chicago White Sox, owned by brilliant innovator and future Hall of Famer Bill Veeck, try something new—and dreadful: In the first game of a doubleheader against the Royals on August 8, 1976, White Sox players wear short pants and win, 5–2. (They wore long pants in the second game and lost 7–1.)

ELEMENTARY, WATSON

Bob Watson becomes the fist man to hit for the cycle in both leagues on September 15, 1979 when he does it for the Boston Red Sox. Watson had previously hit for the cycle on June 24, 1977 for the Houston Astros.

A REDS-LETTER DAY

Pete Rose of the Reds smacks the 3,000th hit of his career on May 5, 1978.

IT'S A STRETCH
WILLIE "STRETCH" MCCOVEY OF THE SAN FRANCISCO GIANTS HITS THE 500TH HOME RUN OF HIS CAREER ON JUNE 30, 1978.

That's a wrap!
Pete Rose's 44-game hitting streak, which started on June 14, 1978, ends on July 31, 1978 as he goes 0-for-4 against the Braves, who beat the Reds 16–4.

A FIRST FOR YAZ
Carl Yastrzemski's 3,000th hit makes him the 15th player to hit that mark and the first American Leaguer with 400 home runs and 3,000 hits on September 12, 1979.

SECOND TO 4,000
21 years to the day after his first hit, Pete Rose of the Montreal Expos collects his 4,000th hit, a double off Jerry Koosman of the Phillies on April 13, 1984.

MR. SEPTEMBER
17 years after his first home run, on September 17, 1984, Reggie Jackson of the California Angels hits the 500th home run of his career.

THE HIT KING
Pete Rose of the Reds gets his 4,192nd hit on September 11, 1985, breaking Ty Cobb's all-time career hit record.

FOUR!
Bob Horner of the Braves hits four home runs in a game on July 6, 1986 in Atlanta, but the Expos win 11–8.

STAYIN' ALIVE
Down to his last strike, Dave Henderson of the Red Sox hits a two-run homer with two outs in the ninth inning off Donnie Moore of the Angels in Game 5 of the American League Championship Series on October 12, 1986. The homer gives Boston, who must win to stay alive in the series, a 6–5 lead. The Angels tie the game in the bottom of the inning, but the Red Sox win in the 11th inning. The Sox will win the series 4–3 and go on to face the New York Mets in the World Series.

ABOUT SCHMIDT
Mike Schmidt of the Philadelphia Phillies hits the 500th home run of his career on April 18, 1987 at Three Rivers Stadium in Pittsburgh.

WHAT A CATCH! OUCH!

Ozzie Smith of the Cardinals hits a fly ball that hooks towards foul territory near the left field corner at Busch Stadium in St. Louis on April 26, 1989. Giants outfielder Kevin Mitchell overruns the ball and reaches up to catch it barehanded with his right hand—one of the most memorable catches ever.

A WEIRD MARK FOR KEVIN MAAS

In 1991, Kevin Maas of the New York Yankees reaches an unusual milestone: he's the first player with at least 20 home runs (he had 21) whose RBI total is not twice his home run total. Maas had just 41 RBIs in 1991.

ROCKIN' ROBIN

Robin Yount of the Milwaukee Brewers gets his 3,000th hit on September 9, 1992. Yount becomes just the second player (after Willie Mays) with 3,000 hits, 200 stolen bases, and 100 triples.

HARD HITTIN' WHITEN

MARK WHITEN OF THE CARDINALS TIES MAJOR LEAGUE RECORDS WITH FOUR HOME RUNS AND 12 RUNS BATTED IN ONE GAME AT CINCINNATI ON SEPTEMBER 7, 1993.

SOX SOCKS

Robin Ventura hits two grand slams and drives in eight runs in one game for the Chicago White Sox on September 4, 1995.

STEADY EDDIE

Eddie Murray of the Orioles hits his 500th home run on September 6, 1996.

An inside job

Sammy Sosa of the Cubs and Tony Womack of the Pirates both hit inside the park home runs in the sixth inning on May 26, 1997.

I'll have another Big Mac please

Mark McGwire's 50th home run for the St. Louis Cardinals on August 20, 1998, makes him the first player to hit at least 50 homers in three consecutive years.

61 IN '98

Mark McGwire of the Cardinals hits his 61st home run of the season on September 7, 1998, to tie Roger Maris's record.

62!

Four Cardinal Hall of Famers are on hand as Mark McGwire hits his 62nd home run of the season, breaking the record set by Roger Maris in 1961. Stan Musial, Ozzie Smith, Lou Brock, and Red Schoendienst watch the historic blast with Maris's family at Busch Stadium in St. Louis on September 9, 1998.

THEY'RE GONE!

Mark McGwire of the Cardinals hits his final home runs of the season, #69 and #70 on September 27, 1998.

JOSÉ LEADS THE WAY

José Canseco of the Tampa Bay Devil Rays, a native of Havana, Cuba, smacks the 400th home run of his career on April 14, 1999—the first foreign-born player to reach that mark.

MAC ATTACK

Mark McGwire of the St. Louis Cardinals connects for the 500th home run of his career, on August 5, 1999, one year after he hit his 400th. Incredible.

MAKING THEM COUNT

In 1999, Mark McGwire of the Cardinals becomes the first player with at least 100 hits to have more RBIs (147) than hits (145).

BACK FOR MORE

Mo Vaughn, Tim Salmon, and Troy Glaus of the Anaheim Angels all homer in the fourth inning against Dwight Gooden of the Tampa Bay Devil Rays on April 22, 2000. The same three homer again off Roberto Hernandez in the ninth, marking the first time three players homered in the same inning twice in one game.

MAKING THE ROUNDS
Tampa Bay Devil Ray slugger Fred McGriff hits a home run on August 26, 2000, at Camden Yards in Baltimore. That's the record 37th ballpark he's homered in.

IN GOOD COMPANY
BARRY BONDS HITS THE 500TH HOME RUN OF HIS CAREER IN SAN FRANCISCO ON APRIL 17, 2001. WILLIE MAYS (660) AND WILLIE MCCOVEY (521) HELP BONDS CELEBRATE.

BY BONDS!
Barry Bonds of the San Francisco Giants hits his record-breaking 71st and 72nd home runs of the season on October 5, 2001 against the Dodgers. He will extend his record to 73 by the end of the season.

THAT'S A LOT OF RUNS!
The ageless Rickey Henderson (42) of the San Diego Padres breaks Ty Cobb's record for most runs scored in a career, when he crosses the plate with run #2,246 on October 4, 2001. Cobb's record had stood for 73 years.

A SECOND FATHER AND SON GAME
Tim Raines, Sr. and Jr. play in the same game as outfielders for the Baltimore Orioles on October 4, 2001 against the Red Sox.

HENDERSON REACHES 3,000 AND IT'S NOT HIS AGE

41-year-old Rickey Henderson of the San Diego Padres (one of the few players to bat righty and throw lefty) smacks his 3,000th hit, a double on October 7, 2001. The game also marks the final game for teammate Tony Gwynn (3,141 hits).

GOING, GOING, GOING, GOING, GONE!

On May 23, 2002, Shawn Green of the Los Angeles Dodgers hits four homers in a game against the Milwaukee Brewers at Miller Park. He adds a single and a double in his 6-for-6 day, and winds up with a record 19 total bases.

DEMON DAMON

Johnny Damon of the Boston Red Sox becomes the second man in history to have three hits in one inning (a double, triple, and single in the first) on June 27, 2003 against the Florida Marlins.

BARRY, BARRY GOOD

BARRY BONDS HITS THE 600TH HOME RUN OF HIS CAREER ON AUGUST 9, 2002.

SHOW ME A TEAM, I'LL HIT YOU A HOMER

Todd Zeile homers for the New York Yankees on April 2, 2003. This marks a record 10th team for which Zeile has homered. Previously, he homered for the Cardinals, Cubs, Phillies, Orioles, Dodgers, Marlins, Rangers, Mets, and Rockies.

Slammin' Sammy

Sammy Sosa of the Cubs hits his 500th home run on April 4, 2003.

WHAT, ANOTHER BARRY BONDS HOME RUN MOMENT?

Barry Bonds of the San Francisco Giants smacks the 661st home run of his career on April 13, 2004, at SBC Park, passing his godfather Willie Mays, and moving into third place on the all-time home run list, behind only Babe Ruth and Hank Aaron.

FOUR GONE

MIKE CAMERON OF THE MARINERS HITS FOUR HOME RUNS IN A GAME ON MAY 2, 2003.

VIVA RAFFY!

Rafael Palmeiro of the Texas Rangers hits the 500th home run of his career on May 11, 2003.

BIG DAY FOR BIG CARLOS

Carlos Delgado of the Toronto Blue Jays hits four home runs in a game on September 25, 2003. The first was Delgado's 300th career homer.

Oldie but goodie

Julio Franco of the Braves smacks a pinch-hit home run in Atlanta on May 19, 2004. At 45, he's the oldest man ever to do so.

JUNIOR JOLT

Ken Griffey, Jr. of the Cincinnati Reds connects for the 500th home run of his career on June 20, 2004.

700 AND COUNTING

On September 17, 2004, Barry Bonds hit the 700th home run of his career at home in San Francisco.

I didn't know that

"You never know what you're going to see at the ballpark."
Unattributed

TALK ABOUT A HIGH POP-UP!

Catcher Gabby Street of the Washington Nationals (Senators) catches a ball dropped 555 feet from the top of the Washington Monument on August 21, 1908. The prize? $500.

THIS UMP WAS A PLAYER

Bill Dinneen, who played in the 1903 World Series for the Boston Pilgrims, has switched careers and is now an umpire. On October 14, 1911, in the first game of the World Series between the As and the Giants, Dinneen becomes the first man to play and later to umpire in the Series.

AN INFAMOUS TRICK PLAY

Miller Huggins, manager of the St. Louis Cardinals, is coaching third base on August 7, 1915, as was common at the time. With a runner on base, Huggins asks the Brooklyn pitcher, rookie Ed Appleton, to throw him the ball. When the pitcher obliges, Huggins jumps out of the way, and while the Brooklyn players scramble for the ball, the St. Louis runner scores. The rules are soon changed to outlaw this hilarious but unsportsmanlike play.

A tough man to whiff

Joe Sewell strikes out twice in one game. Stop the presses. Sewell is still recognized as the toughest man in baseball to strike out. Sewell, a future Hall of Famer, had only two multiple-strikeout games during his 14-year big league career. The first was on May 13, 1923. The second two-strikeout game for Sewell was on May 26, 1930.

THE IRON MAN OF 1930

Chuck Klein of the Phillies plays in every inning of every game during the 1930 season—except for one, on July 24, 1930. Klein argues a strikeout call with umpire Lou Jorda in the eighth inning, and is ejected.

WHAT ARE THE ODDS?

The game between the Phillies and the Cubs on July 1, 1931 features both a triple play and Chuck Klein hitting for the cycle.

YOU ARE OUT! TWICE!

New York Giants manager Mel Ott sets a dubious—but unbreakable—record on June 9, 1946, when he becomes the first manager to be ejected from both games of a doubleheader.

THESE CLEATS ARE MADE FOR WALKING
THE NEW YORK YANKEES WALKED 11 TIMES IN THE THIRD INNING VS. THE WASHINGTON SENATORS ON SEPTEMBER 11, 1949.

Your attention please. now playing first base for the Yankees, Joe DiMaggio
Joe DiMaggio plays his only game at first base on July 3, 1950. In the next game, it's back to the outfield.

A TOUGH BREAK FOR TED WILLIAMS
TED WILLIAMS BREAKS HIS LEFT ELBOW IN THE FIRST INNING OF THE JULY 11, 1950 ALL-STAR GAME IN CHICAGO.

A BIG DAY FOR PEE WEE
Harold "Pee Wee" Reese reaches base three times in the first inning—including two walks—on May 21, 1952. He's the only National Leaguer to do so in the 20th century.

YOU CAN GO HOME

On September 25, the last day of the 1955 season, the New York Giants host the Phillies for a double-header. In the second game, with Philadelphia ahead 3–1 in the bottom of the ninth inning, Joey Amalfitano is on second with Whitey Lockman on first. Bobby Hofman then lines to Ted Kazanski at short (one out). He throws to Bobby Morgan at second to get Amalfitano (two), who relays the ball to Marv Blaylock at first to get Lockman. Triple play. Game over. Season over.

How else can I catch a knuckleball?

On May 27, 1960, catcher Clint Courtney of the Baltimore Orioles uses a giant catcher's mitt to catch knuckleballer Hoyt Wilhelm and cut down on passed balls. The mitt is one and a half times as large as a standard mitt. Courtney has no passed balls as the Orioles beat the Yankees 3–2.

BILL VEECK IS AT IT AGAIN

Responding to complaints that vendors were blocking the view of fans at Comiskey Park, White Sox owner Bill Veeck, baseball's consummate showman hires eight midgets, including Eddie Gaedel, to work the box seats for the home opener, April 19, 1961.

STOP THE WORLD, I WANT TO GET OFF

After the Red Sox lose 13–3 to the Yankees on July 26, 1962, Gene Conley and Elijah "Pumpsie" Green bolt the Sox team bus. Conley winds up at Idlewild Airport (later JFK) trying to buy a ticket to fly to Israel. But he has no visa. Green returns to the team two days later and is fined for being AWOL.

THE FIRST AND LAST

The first annual Hispanic American All-Star Game is played on October 12, 1963 at the Polo Grounds in New York. Juan Marichal, Manny Mota, Pedro Ramos, Tony Oliva, Roberto Clemente, Zoilo Versalles, Vic Power, Luis Aparicio, Felipe Alou, and Minnie Minoso participate. The National League team wins 5–2. This game is also the last annual Hispanic American All-Star Game.

Save situation

Frank Robinson falls in a pool on August 22, 1966 and is saved from drowning by teammate Andy Etchebarren.

HOW TO MESS UP A SCORECARD

Cesar Tovar of the Twins plays all nine positions on September 22, 1968. The first batter he faces in the first inning is Bert Campaneris, who had also accomplished this feat.

TRENDSETTER

ON APRIL 15, 1972, REGGIE JACKSON OF THE OAKLAND ATHLETICS TAKES THE FIELD WITH A MUSTACHE—THE FIRST BIG LEAGUER WITH FACIAL HAIR SINCE WALLY SCHANG IN 1914.

NOT THAT KIND OF BATS

The Reds-Expos game in Cincinnati is stopped in the sixth inning on August 22, 1979, but not because Johnny Bench has hit his 325th career homer, breaking Frank Robinson's Reds record. No, the game is stopped because bats (the flying mammal kind) landed on the field and were removed by the grounds crew.

AN OUT AND OUT CHEAT

Instead of being banned from the game for life, Seattle Mariners manager Maury Wills is suspended for a whopping two games after ordering the grounds crew at the Kingdome to enlarge the batter's box by a foot on April 25, 1981, giving his batters a better chance to hit breaking balls. Wills is fired on May 6.

HOW MUCH DO YOU LOVE YOUR MUSTACHE?

On February 21, 1986, Rollie Fingers declines to sign with the Cincinnati Reds and extend his Hall of Fame career because he'd have to shave his trademark handlebar mustache to comply with owner Marge Schott's edict about facial hair.

Roger and out

Home plate umpire Terry Cooney ejects Boston pitcher Roger Clemens from Game 4 of the 1990 American League Championship Series on October 10 for cursing at him and for threatening to "get" umpire Jim Evans. (History does not record which words were used.) Oakland wins the game 3–1, and sweeps the Sox 4–0. Clemens is fined $10,000 and suspended for the first five games in 1991.

WHAT WAS THE FINAL SCORE?

The New York Mets beat the Atlanta Braves on October 18, 1999 in Game 5 of the National League Championship Series. The final score of the game is either 7–3, 5–3, or 4–3. With the bases loaded (Roger Cedeño on third, John Olerud on second, and Todd Pratt on first base) in the bottom of the 15th inning, Robin Ventura of the Mets hits a Kevin McGlinchy pitch over the fence for what appears to be a walk-off grand slam. Cedeño and Olerud scores. But Pratt, running from first, stops near third base, then retreats towards second to congratulate Ventura behind the base. The field is cleared, the umpires leave, and the Mets celebrate their dramatic victory. But Pratt never touched the plate. Nor did Ventura. Red Foley, the official scorer, decides that Cedeño's run ended the game. So Ventura homered into a double, and although Olerud touched the plate, his run doesn't count. Final score: 4–3.

THE INCREDIBLE ICHIRO

In 2001, his rookie season with the Seattle Mariners, Ichiro Suziki turns a very rare double: He is named both Rookie of the Year and Most Valuable Player in the American League. With the permission of the league, the name on the back of his uniform is his first, not his last name.

Beating the odds

Travis Phelps makes his major league debut with the Tampa Bay Devil Rays on April 19, 2001. Taken in the 89th round of the 1996 draft, Phelps is the lowest-round draft pick ever to make the majors. He pitches in 79 games.

Pitching

*"Sandy's fastball was
so fast, some batters
would start to swing as
he was on his way to
the mound."*

Jim Murray, about Sandy Koufax

USING HIS NOODLE

Frank "Noodles" Hahn of the Cincinnati Reds no-hits the Philadelphia Phillies 4–0 on July 12, 1900.

A GIANT EFFORT BY MATTY

Christy Mathewson of the New York Giants throws the first no-hitter of his career, a 5–0 victory over the St. Louis Cardinals on July 15, 1901.

NIX ON THE HITS

James "Nixey" Callahan of the Chicago White Sox pitches a 3–0 no-hitter against the Detroit Tigers on September 20, 1902, the first no-hitter in the American League.

"Iron Man" Joe McGinnity I

"Iron Man" Joe McGinnity of the New York Giants wins both games of a doubleheader against the Boston Braves, August 1, 1903.

"IRON MAN" JOE MCGINNITY II

"Iron Man" Joe McGinnity of the Giants wins both games of a doubleheader for the second time in a month, beating the Dodgers on August 8, 1903.

"IRON MAN" JOE MCGINNITY III

"Iron Man" Joe McGinnity of the Giants wins both games of a doubleheader against the Phillies on August 31, 1903. This marks the third time in a month in which he has won both games of a twin bill.

> *HOT CHICK*
>
> *Charles "Chick" Fraser of the Philadelphia Phillies no-hits the Chicago Cubs 10–0 on September 18, 1903.*

A PERFECT GAME FOR CY YOUNG

Cy Young pitches a perfect game for the Boston Red Sox, shutting out the Philadelphia Athletics 3–0 on May 5, 1904.

KNOCKING THEIR SOX OFF

Jesse Tannehill of the Boston Red Sox no-hits the Chicago White Sox 6–0 on August 17, 1904.

NO WONDER HE'S HAPPY

New York Highlanders pitcher "Happy" Jack Chesbro notches his 41st victory of the season on October 7, 1904. It's a record that will probably stand for all time.

NUMBER TWO FOR BIG SIX
Christy Mathewson of the Giants throws his
second no-hitter on June 13, 1905, as the Giants
beat the Cubs 1–0.

WELL DONE, WELDON

Weldon Henley of the Philadelphia As pitches a
no-hitter and beats the St. Louis Browns 6–0 on
July 22, 1905.

TURNING THE TIGERS INTO PUSSYCATS

FRANK SMITH OF THE CHICAGO WHITE SOX NO-HITS
THE DETROIT TIGERS ON SEPTEMBER 6, 1905 IN A
15–0 BLOWOUT.

BIG BILL SHUTS THEM DOWN

Bill Dinneen of the Boston Red Sox throws a 2–0
no-hitter against the Chicago White Sox on September
27, 1905.

LUSH LIFE

*Johnny Lush of the Philadelphia Phillies throws
a 6–0 no-hitter against the Brooklyn Dodgers,
May 1, 1906.*

BIG DAY FOR BIG JEFF

"Big Jeff" Pfeffer (real name Francis Xavier) has a big
game—a no-hitter for the Boston Braves against the
Cincinnati Reds on May 8, 1907.

NICKED

NICK MADDOX OF THE PITTSBURGH PIRATES
PITCHES A NO-HITTER AGAINST THE DODGERS
ON SEPTEMBER 20, 1907.

CY STRIKES AGAIN

Cy Young throws his second no-hitter of the
20th century on June 30, 1908, as Boston shuts
out New York 8–0.

A JULY 4 TO REMEMBER

George "Hooks" Wiltse of the Giants no-hits the Philadelphia Phillies on July 4, 1908.

> ### NAP TIME
>
> *George "Nap" Rucker of Crabapple, Georgia, throws a no-hitter for the Brooklyn Dodgers, who beat the Boston Braves 6–0 on September 5, 1908.*

A TOUGH RHOADES TO HOE

The Cleveland Indians' Bob "Dusty" Rhoades no-hits the Boston Red Sox on September 18, 1908.

Do it again

Frank Smith of the White Sox pitches his second no-hitter, beating the Philadelphia Athletics 1–0 on September 20, 1908.

ADDIE BOY!

CLEVELAND'S ADDIE JOSS THROWS A PERFECT GAME AGAINST CHICAGO, OCTOBER 2, 1908.

ANOTHER NO-HITTER FOR ADDIE JOSS

Cleveland's Addie Joss throws his second no-hitter on April 20, 1910.

Super Chief
Charles Albert "Chief" Bender of the Philadelphia As no-hits Cleveland 4–0 on May 12, 1910.

SMOKED
"Smokey" Joe Wood of the Boston Red Sox throws a 5–0 no-hitter against the St. Louis Browns on July 29, 1911.

◆ --

BIG ED'S NO-NO
Ed Walsh of the White Sox throws a 5–0 no-hitter against the Red Sox on August 27, 1911.

THE END OF AN UNFORGETTABLE CAREER
Cy Young of the Boston Braves wins the 511th and final game of his career on September 22, 1911, at the age of 44.

Happy birthday!
George Mullin of the Tigers pitches a no-hitter against the St. Louis Browns on his birthday, July 4, 1912.

THAT'S EARL, FOLKS
Earl Hamilton of the Browns no-hits the Detroit Tigers on August 30, 1912.

PHILLIE-BUSTER
Jeff Tesreau of the Giants no-hits the Phillies 3–0 on September 6, 1912.

First brother battery
New York Highlanders pitcher Tommy Thompson and catcher Homer Thompson form the first brother battery in the majors on October 14, 1912.

No home towners to see his debut
Ed Porray makes his big league debut pitching for the Buffalo Buffeds in the Federal League (considered a major league) on April 17, 1914. But there's nobody from his hometown at the ballpark to see his first game, because he doesn't have a hometown. He was born at sea.

GIVING THEM THE BENZ
Joe Benz of the White Sox fires a no-hitter to beat the Cleveland Indians on May 31, 1914.

LET GEORGE DO IT
George Davis of the Boston Braves no-hits the Phillies 7–0 on September 9, 1914.

Marquard's no-hitter
Richard "Rube" Marquard of the Giants no-hits the Dodgers 2–0 on April 15, 1915.

LAVENDER IS NOT BLUE
JIMMY LAVENDER PITCHES A NO-HITTER ON AUGUST 31, 1915 FOR THE CHICAGO CUBS, BEATING THE NEW YORK GIANTS 2–0.

TOM HUGHES'S NO-HITTER
Boston Braves' pitcher Tom Hughes pitches a no-hitter on June 16, 1916 to beat the Pirates 2–0.

RUBE'S GEM
George "Rube" Foster of the Red Sox no-hits the Yankees 2–0 on June 21, 1916.

SPEEDING BULLET
The Philadelphia As' "Bullet" Joe Bush throws a 5–0 no-hitter against the Cleveland Indians on August 26, 1916.

DUTCH MASTER
HUBERT "DUTCH" LEONARD OF THE BOSTON RED SOX NO-HITS THE ST. LOUIS BROWNS ON AUGUST 30, 1916.

KNUCKLING UNDER
Eddie "Knuckles" Cicotte—who would be banned from baseball as one of the Black Sox in 1919—throws a no-hitter for the Chicago White Sox on April 14, 1917.

ANOTHER NO-HITTER, 10 DAYS LATER
The Yankees' George Mogridge no-hits the Red Sox on April 24, 1917.

A DOUBLE NO-HITTER
Hippo Vaughn of the Cubs and Fred Toney of the Reds throw no-hitters for nine innings in the same game on May 2, 1917. Toney wins the game 1–0 in ten innings.

KOOB'S NO BOOB

Ernie Koob of the St. Louis Browns pitches a no-hitter to beat the White Sox 1–0 on May 5, 1917.

Another day, another no-hitter

Bob Groom of the St. Louis Browns pitches a no-hitter against the Chicago White Sox in the second game of a doubleheader on May 6, 1917, just one day after his teammate Ernie Koob pitched one.

REPEAT PERFORMANCE

Dutch Leonard of the Red Sox pitches his second no-hitter, a 4–0 victory over the Tigers on June 3, 1918.

PLAYING HOD-BALL

HORACE "HOD" ELLER OF THE CINCINNATI REDS PITCHES A 6–0 NO-HITTER AGAINST THE ST. LOUIS CARDINALS ON MAY 11, 1919.

AN ODD NO-HITTER

Babe Ruth of the Boston Red Sox is the starting pitcher in one of the most unusual games of all time on June 23, 1917. The first batter for the Senators is Ray Morgan. Ruth walks him, then argues the ball four call with home plate umpire Brick Owen. Argues too vociferously, apparently, because Owen ejects Ruth, who is replaced by Ernie Shore. Morgan is thrown out trying to steal second. No other Senator reaches base, and Shore has a 26-batter "perfect game."

RAY OF LIGHT

Cleveland's Ray Caldwell no-hits the Yankees 3–0 on September 10, 1919.

Washington monument

Walter Johnson of the Washington Senators records his 300th win on May 14, 1920.

THE BIG TRAIN ROLLS ON

Walter Johnson of the Washington Senators throws a no-hitter against the Boston Red Sox on July 1, 1920.

A perfect day
Charlie Robertson of the White Sox pitches a perfect game against the Tigers on April 30, 1922.

BARNES-BURNER
Jesse Barnes throws a 6–0 no-hitter for the Giants against the Phillies on May 7, 1922.

SAM'S CLUB
"SAD" SAM JONES OF THE YANKEES NO-HITS THE PHILADELPHIA ATHLETICS ON SEPTEMBER 4, 1923.

COMING UP EHMKE
The Red Sox's Howard Ehmke fires a no-hitter on September 7, 1923.

NOT SO BRAVE
Cardinals pitcher Jesse Haines no-hits the Boston Braves on July 17, 1924.

A DIZZYING GAME FOR DAZZY
Clarence "Dazzy" Vance of the Dodgers, from Orient, Iowa, no-hits the Phillies 10–1 on September 13, 1925.

TED LYONS THROWS A NO-HITTER
Ted Lyons of the Chicago White Sox throws a 6–0 no-hit victory over the Boston Red Sox. August 21, 1926.

HUBBELL HOBBLES THE PIRATES
Carl Hubbell throws a no-hitter for the Giants against the Pirates on May 8, 1929.

BROWNOUT
Wes Ferrell of the Indians no-hits the Browns 9–0 on April 29, 1931.

CAPITAL GAIN
WASHINGTON SENATORS PITCHER BOBBY BURKE FIRES A NO-HITTER TO BEAT THE RED SOX 5–0 ON AUGUST 8, 1931.

KING CARL'S INCREDIBLE PITCHING PERFORMANCE

In the second All-Star game, played at the Polo Grounds in New York on July 10, 1934, Carl Hubbell turns in one of the most amazing pitching performances ever. With Charlie Gehringer and Heinie Manush on base in the first inning and no outs, Hubbell strikes out Babe Ruth, Lou Gehrig, and Jimmie Foxx to end the inning. In the second, Hubbell strikes out two more future Hall of Famers—Al Simmons and Joe Cronin: five in a row.

THE DEAN OF NO-HITTERS
Paul Dean of the Cardinals pitches 3–0 a no-hitter against the Dodgers on September 21, 1934.

Bill Klem's no-hitters
Hall of Fame umpire Bill Klem goes 27 years and a day between no-hitters. His first was on September 20, 1907, when Nick Maddox of the Pirates no-hit Brooklyn 2–0. Klem did his second and last no-hitter on September 21, 1934, when Paul "Daffy" Dean of the St. Louis Cardinals no-hit the Dodgers 3–0.

HEY, VERN
VERN KENNEDY OF THE WHITE SOX NO-HITS THE
INDIANS 5–0 ON AUGUST 31, 1935.

AN AUSPICIOUS START
In the first start of his major league career,
17-year-old Bob Feller of the Cleveland Indians
strikes out 15 St. Louis Browns on August 23, 1936.

WHAT DID *YOU* DO WHILE *YOU* WERE IN HIGH SCHOOL?
In his fifth career start, Bob Feller of the
Cleveland Indians strikes out his age—17
Philadelphia Athletics on September 13, 1936.
When the season ends, Feller returns home to
Van Meter, Iowa to finish high school.

Bill Dietrich's game to remember
White Sox pitcher Bill Dietrich no-hits the
Browns 8–0 on June 1, 1937.

Bad break

In one of baseball's most infamous injuries, Earl Averill of the Cleveland Indians hits a ball right off a toe on Dizzy Dean's left foot in the third inning of the July 7, 1937 All-Star Game at Griffith Stadium in Washington, D.C. The Cardinals' pitching star's toe is broken. Dean comes back too soon, changes his pitching motion to accommodate his toe, and suffers a torn rotator cuff, significantly shortening his career.

THAT'S #1

Johnny Vander Meer of the Cincinnati Reds pitches a no-hitter against the Boston Braves, winning 3–0 on June 11, 1938.

THAT'S #2

In his next start after his first no-hitter, Johnny Vander Meer pitches another no-hitter on June 15, 1938, in the first night game in Brooklyn, shutting out the Dodgers 6–0—the only consecutive no-hitters in history.

FULL MONTE

Montgomery Marcellus Pearson, known as "Monte" or "Hoot" fires a no-hitter for the Yankees to beat the Indians 13–0 on August 27, 1938.

WHAT AN OPENING DAY

On April 16, 1940, Cleveland's Bob Feller pitches a no-hitter and beats the Chicago White Sox 1–0 —the only Opening Day no-hitter in the majors.

TEX LEAVES THEM SEEING RED

James "Tex" Carleton of Comanche, Texas, throws a no-hitter for the Brooklyn Dodgers against the Reds in Cincinnati on April 30, 1940.

Now pitching, Ted Williams

Ted Williams pitches the last two innings of a 12–1 Boston loss to the Detroit Tigers on August 24, 1940. He strikes out Rudy York. The catcher is Joe Glenn, who had caught Babe Ruth's last game on the mound in 1933.

HUM BABY!

Lon Warneke, "The Arkansas Hummingbird," throws a no-hitter for the St. Louis Cardinals on August 30, 1941 against the Reds in Cincinnati.

DODGE 'EM

Jim Tobin of the Boston Braves no-hits the Brooklyn Dodgers on April 27, 1944.

SHOUN' THEM HOW

Clyde Shoun of the Reds fires a no-hit game against the Boston Braves on May 15, 1944.

HE'S HOW OLD?

Joe Nuxhall is just 15 on June 10, 1944, when he pitches ⅔ of an inning for the Cincinnati Reds in relief—the youngest player ever to appear in a major league game.

AN HEROIC DEBUT

BERT SHEPARD, WHO LOST HIS RIGHT FOOT IN WORLD WAR II, PITCHES 5⅓ INNINGS FOR THE WASHINGTON SENATORS ON AUGUST 4, 1945.

NOW PITCHING, JIMMIE FOXX

Jimmie Foxx, a future Hall of Famer and a member of the 500 home run club, starts for the Philadelphia Phillies (known as the Blue Jays at the time) and pitches seven innings on August 19, 1945. Foxx gets the win—the only one of his career.

Rapid return
After 44 months of naval combat, Bob Feller returns to the mound in Cleveland, striking out 12 Tigers on August 24, 1945.

NO HITTER, EH?

Toronto native Dick Fowler throws a 1–0 no-hitter for the Philadelphia As on September 9, 1945.

HEAD'S UP

Ed Head, owner of one of the great rhyming names of all time, throws a no-hitter for the Brooklyn Dodgers to shut out the Boston Braves on April 23, 1946.

I'LL SECOND THAT
Bob Feller of the Cleveland Indians throws his second no-hitter on April 30, 1946 to beat the Yankees 1–0.

THE EEPHUS PITCH

You won't find it in most dictionaries, and if you are not a baseball fan, you'll think it's a typographical error or a Dr. Seuss creation. But the Eephus pitch was the specialty of pitcher Rip Sewell. The pitch is a giant, slo-pitch style arc ball which takes about eight minutes to reach home plate. Sewell never surrendered a home run when he threw it until the bottom of the eighth inning of the July 9, 1946 All-Star Game at Fenway Park. Ted Williams hit it into the bullpen as the American League romped 12–0.

> *WHIPPED*
> *Ewell "The Whip" Blackwell of the Reds throws a no-hitter against the Boston Braves on June 18, 1947.*

BLACKOUT

Don Black of the Indians no-hits the Philadelphia As on July 10, 1947.

A FIRST FOR DAN BANKHEAD

Dan Bankhead is the first black man to pitch in the modern major leagues when he makes his mound debut for the Brooklyn Dodgers on August 26, 1947.

A hometown no-hitter

Philadelphia native Bill McCahan pitches a no-hitter for the Philadelphia As on September 3, 1947 in Philadelphia.

FIRST AMERICAN LEAGUE NO-HITTER AT NIGHT

Cleveland's Bob Lemon pitches the first no-hitter at night in the American League on June 30, 1948, beating the Tigers 2–0.

Don't look back

Satchel Paige makes his major league debut pitching for the Cleveland Indians. July 9, 1948. Paige is approximately 42 years old at the time. He remains the oldest rookie in major league history. His six victories in 1948 help the Indians win the American League pennant. Paige had been one of the biggest stars of the Negro Leagues, but was barred from playing in the majors during his prime. He pitched for the Indians, the Browns, and the Kansas City Athletics.

IT'S A NO-HITTER!

Rex Barney of the Brooklyn Dodgers no-hits the New York Giants on June 9, 1948.

Bickford makes Dodgers blue

Vern Bickford of the Braves throws a no-hitter against the Dodgers on August 11, 1950.

CLIFF-HANGER

The Pirates' Cliff Chambers no-hits the Boston Braves on May 6, 1951.

VOLUME THREE

The Indians' Bob Feller throws his third no-hitter on July 1, 1951, a victory over the Tigers in the first game of a doubleheader.

FIRST OF TWO

Allie Reynolds of the New York Yankees— "Superchief"—throws a no-hitter against the Indians on July 12, 1951.

ENCORE

On September 28, 1951, Allie Reynolds of the Yankees becomes the first American Leaguer to pitch two no-hitters in the same season, as he beats the Red Sox 8–0.

FIRED UP
Virgil "Fire" Trucks of the Tigers no-hits the
Washington Senators 1–0 on May 15, 1952.

BAD NEWS, BEARS
Carl Erskine, known in Brooklyn as "Oisk," throws
a no-hitter for the Dodgers to beat the Chicago
Cubs 5–0 on June 19, 1952.

HE DID IT AGAIN
VIRGIL TRUCKS DOES IT AGAIN—HIS SECOND
NO-HITTER OF THE SEASON ON AUGUST 25, 1952,
AS THE TIGERS BEAT THE YANKEES 1–0.

NOW PITCHING, STAN MUSIAL
*Future Hall of Famer Stan "The Man" Musial, who has
secured the National League batting crown for the
sixth time, makes his pitching debut for the St. Louis
Cardinals on September 29, 1952. The batter is
Frankie Baumholtz of the Cubs, who finished second
to Musial. For the first time in his career, Baumholtz
bats righty, and reaches on an error.*

FIRST START, FIRST NO-HITTER

Alva Lee "Bobo" Holloman pitches a no-hitter for the St. Louis Browns on May 6, 1953, in his first major league start—the only man to accomplish this feat. He is demoted to the minors later in the season.

MILWAUKEE'S FIRST

Jim Wilson of the Milwaukee Braves no-hits the Phillies on June 12, 1954.

A HAPPY DAY FOR SAD SAM JONES

"Sad" Sam Jones pitches a no-hitter for the Cubs over the Pirates on May 12, 1955. "Toothpick" Jones is not related to the Sam Jones who pitched a no-hitter for the Yankees to beat the Philadelphia As on September 4, 1923, but the Joneses become the first pitchers with the same first and last name to pitch no-hitters.

CUTTING THE GIANTS DOWN TO SIZE

It's a second no-hitter for Carl Erskine of the Brooklyn Dodgers on May 12, 1956, a 3–0 victory over the Giants.

MELODIOUS
Mel Parnell of the Red Sox fires a 4–0 no-hitter to beat the White Sox on July 14, 1956.

A close shave
Sal "The Barber" Maglie (so named because his inside pitches seemed to shave the batters) throws a no-hitter for the Dodgers, a 5–0 win over the Phillies on September 25, 1956.

THE FIRST CY YOUNG AWARD
The first Cy Young Award for pitching excellence is presented in 1956, the year after Young's death. The first winner is Don Newcombe of the Brooklyn Dodgers: 27–7 with an ERA of 3.06. During the first 11 years of its existence, one award is given. Starting in 1967, a separate award is given in each league.

WHY DO YOU THINK THEY CALL HIM SMILEY?

Bob "Smiley" Keegan of the White Sox fires a no-hitter to beat the Senators 6–0 on August 20, 1957.

A GREAT DAY FOR THE HONORABLE GENTLEMAN FROM KENTUCKY

Future Senator (United States Senator [R-Kentucky] in Washington, not Washington Senator) Jim Bunning pitches his first no-hitter, on July 20, 1958, to lead his Tigers to a 3–0 victory over the Red Sox.

Hoyt Wilhelm's Gem

Hoyt Wilhelm did not start a game during his first six years and 185 games in the majors (1952–1957). In 1958 he started a total of 10 games for the Indians and the Orioles. On September 20, 1958, Wilhelm was magnificent—firing a no-hitter for Baltimore against the Yankees.

WEIRDEST GAME OF ALL TIME

Pittsburgh Pirates pitcher Harvey Haddix retires the first 36 Milwaukee Braves batters on May 26, 1959. After he finishes the ninth inning, having retired 27 Braves in a row, Haddix sets a new record with each successive Brave he retires, for no one before has ever pitched a perfect game beyond the ninth inning. But the Pirates can't score a run. In the 13th inning, Felix Mantilla reaches base on an error by third baseman Don Hoak. A sacrifice moves Mantilla to second base. Hank Aaron is walked intentionally, and Joe Adcock slams a home run—later ruled a double—because Adcock passes Aaron on the bases. So although Haddix pitches a perfect game for 12 innings, he loses it 1–0, in one of the most incredible games of all time.

A Cardinal sin

Don Cardwell of the Cubs throws a 4–0 no-hitter against the Cardinals on May 15, 1960.

LEW'S TURN

Milwaukee's Lew Burdette no-hits the Phillies 1–0 on August 18, 1960.

SPAHN'S FIRST

Warren Spahn of the Milwaukee Braves throws his first no-hitter on September 16, 1960 to beat the Phillies 4–0.

> *REPLAY*
>
> *Warren Spahn of the Braves throws his second no-hitter on April 28, 1961, a 1–0 victory over the Giants.*

A West Coast first

Robert "Bo" Belinsky of the Los Angeles Angels throws the first no-hitter on the West Coast, a 2–0 victory over the Orioles at Dodger Stadium on May 5, 1962.

First by a black pitcher

Earl Wilson of the Red Sox no-hits the Angels 2–0 on June 26, 1962.

NOT THE LAST

Sandy Koufax (born Sanford Braun) throws his first no-hitter for the Dodgers, June 30, 1962.

A NO-NO FOR MONBO
Bill Monbouquette (6 vowels) pitches a no-hitter for the Red Sox to beat the White Sox 1–0 on August 1, 1962.

JACKED UP
THE TWINS' JACK KRALICK NO-HITS THE KANSAS CITY ATHLETICS 1–0 ON AUGUST 26, 1962.

THAT'S A LOT OF Ks
Tom Cheney of the Washington Senators sets the modern record by striking out 21 batters in one game, a 16-inning victory over the Baltimore Orioles on September 12, 1962.

Sandy's second
Sandy Koufax of the Dodgers throws his second no-hitter, an 8–0 beating of the Giants on May 11, 1963.

HOUSTON, WE HAVE LIFTOFF
The Houston Colt .45s' (later the Astros) Don Nottebart throws a 4–1 no-hitter against the Philadelphia Phillies on May 17, 1963.

A NO-HITTER
Future Hall of Famer Juan Marichal of the Giants
no-hits Houston 1–0 on June 15, 1963.

AN EARLY MILESTONE
EARLY WYNN OF THE INDIANS GETS HIS 300TH AND
FINAL WIN ON JULY 13, 1963.

Third in three years
Sandy Koufax of the Dodgers throws his third
no-hitter, resulting in a 3–0 victory over the
Phillies on June 4, 1964.

HAPPY FATHER'S DAY. YOU'RE PERFECT!
Jim Bunning of the Phillies pitches a perfect game
on Father's Day, June 21, 1964. The father of seven
becomes the first man to pitch no-hitters in both
leagues as he beats the Mets 6–0.

JIM PALMER'S FIRST WIN
In the first win of his career, Cooperstown-
bound Jim Palmer of the Baltimore Orioles
beats the Yankees 7–5 on May 16, 1965.
Palmer also blasts a 2-run homer to defeat
Jim Bouton.

EXTRA SPECIAL
The Reds' Jim Maloney no-hits the Chicago
Cubs 1–0 in 10 innings on August 19, 1965.

Perfect!

On September 9, 1965, Sandy Koufax of the Los Angeles Dodgers throws a perfect game, his fourth career no-hitter. Bob Hendley of the Cubs allows just one run—unearned. In the fifth inning, Lou Johnson walks, is sacrificed to second, steals third, and scores on an error. Johnson doubles in the seventh. This is the first game in history with just one hit.

DAVE MOREHEAD ALLOWS NO MORE HITS

Dave Morehead of the Boston Red Sox fires a 2–0 no-hitter against the Chicago White Sox on September 16, 1965.

SONNY DAY

Wilfred "Sonny" Seibert of the Indians no-hits the Washington Senators 2–0 on June 10, 1966.

TWO PITCHERS, ONE NO-HITTER, ONE LOSS

Steve Barber and Stu Miller of the Baltimore Orioles throw nine innings (8.2 for Barber and 0.1 for Miller) of no-hit ball but lose to the Detroit Tigers 2–1 on April 30, 1967. In the top of the ninth inning, with the Orioles ahead 1–0, Dick Tracewski runs for Norm Cash, who has walked. Then Ray Oyler walks, moving Tracewski to second. Jake Wood runs for Oyler. After Willie Horton fouls out, Barber throws a wild pitch, scoring Tracewski and moving Wood to third. Miller replaces Barber on the mound. Wood scores when Don Wert reaches on a fielder's choice that was mishandled by second baseman Mark Belanger.

WILSON BURNS ATLANTA
Don Wilson of the Astros pitches a no-hitter against the Braves, June 18, 1967.

A NO-HITTER BY CHANCE
Dean Chance of the Twins pitches a 2–1 no-hitter against the Cleveland Indians on August 25, 1967.

TIGERS CAGED
The White Sox' Joe Horlen pitches a no-hitter to beat the Tigers 6–0, September 10, 1967.

A PHOEBUS PHENOM

Tom Phoebus of the Orioles no-hits the Red Sox 6–0 on April 27, 1968.

HUNTER'S GEM

Jim "Catfish" Hunter of the Oakland Athletics pitches a perfect game for the Oakland Athletics on May 8, 1968, defeating the Twins 4–0.

A CULVER CLASSIC

GEORGE CULVER PITCHES A 6–1 NO-HITTER FOR THE REDS ON JUNE 29, 1968.

A 30-GAME WINNER

Denny McLain of the Tigers wins his 30th game of the season—becoming the first 30-game winner in 34 years, on September 14, 1968.

SAN FRANCISCO TREAT

Gaylord Perry of the Giants no-hits the Cardinals 1–0 on September 17, 1968.

TURNING THE TABLES

One day after Perry's gem, Ray Washburn of the Cardinals fires a no-hitter to beat the Giants 2–0 on September 18, 1968.

An early highlight

In only the team's ninth game in history, Bill Stoneman of the Expos no-hits the Phillies on April 17, 1969.

HOUSTON, WE HAVE A PROBLEM

Cincinnati's Jim Maloney pitches his second career no-hitter on April 30, 1969 against the Astros.

RETURNING THE FAVOR

The following day, Don Wilson of the Astros no-hits the Reds. Like Maloney, it's his second.

STRAIGHT As

During his 19-year Hall of Fame career, Jim Palmer never gives up a grand slam. On August 13, 1969, Palmer doesn't give up a hit—an 8–0 no-hitter against the Oakland As.

KEN DO!

Ken Holtzman of the Cubs fires a 3–0 no-hitter against the Braves on August 19, 1969.

Moose magic

It's a no-hitter for Bob Moose on September 20, 1969, as his Pirates beat the Mets 4–0.

TEN IN A ROW

Tom Seaver of the New York Mets strikes out a record—an incredible record—ten Padres in a row, April 22, 1970.

FIRST PITCHER IN 1,000 GAMES

When 47-year-old Hoyt Wilhelm throws his first pitch for the Atlanta Braves on May 10, 1970, he becomes the first man to pitch in 1,000 games.

WHAT'S UP, DOCK?

Dock Ellis of the Pirates throws a no-hitter against the Padres, June 12, 1970.

THE WRIGHT STUFF
CLYDE WRIGHT OF THE ANGELS THROWS A
NO-HITTER TO BEAT THE OAKLAND As 4–0 ON
JULY 3, 1970.

L.A. STORY
Bill Singer of the Dodgers throws a 5–0 no-hitter
against the Phillies on July 20, 1970.

HE'S NOT BLUE TODAY
Vida Blue (who turned down $500 from Oakland
As owner Charles O. Finley to change his first
name to "True") pitches a no-hitter for Oakland
on September 21, 1970.

ANOTHER NO-HITTER FOR KEN HOLTZMAN
Ken Holtzman of the Cubs no-hits the Reds 1–0 on
June 3, 1971.

HE CAN HIT, TOO!
*Rick Wise pitches a no-hitter for the
Philadelphia Phillies on June 23, 1971. So
what? Lots of pitchers have thrown no-hitters.
But Wise does something which no other
pitcher has ever done in his own no-hitter:
He hits two home runs in the game, too.*

BOB GIBSON'S ONLY NO-HITTER

Bob Gibson of the Cardinals gets plenty of run support as he no-hits the Pirates 11—0 on August 14, 1971.

LARRY YOUNT'S UNUSUAL CAREER

On September 15, 1971, pitcher Larry Yount (Hall of Famer Robin's brother) is warming up on the mound for the Houston Astros in the ninth inning. Before he can face a batter, he injures his arm and does not pitch in that game or in any other major league game. His career is over.

OF COURSE HE'S HAPPY

Burt "Happy" Hooton throws a no-hitter for the Cubs on April 16, 1972.

One, two, three strikes you're out

Nolan Ryan reaches an amazing milestone: On July 9, 1972 as a member of the California Angels, he strikes out the side on nine pitches. He did the same thing on April 19, 1968 when he was with the Mets. Ryan is the first pitcher to do this in both leagues.

MILT PAPPAS'S GEM

Milt Pappas of the Cubs pitches an 8–0 no-hitter over the San Diego Padres on September 2, 1972.

STONEMAN'S SECOND

Bill Stoneman of the Expos throws his second no-hitter for the Expos over the Mets, October 2, 1972.

A GEM FOR PHIL NIEKRO

Phil Niekro of the Atlanta Braves throws a 9–0 no-hitter on August 5, 1973 to beat the Padres.

BUSBY'S BEAUTY

Steve Busby, a native of beautiful downtown Burbank, California, throws his first no-hitter for the Kansas City Royals to beat the Tigers on April 27, 1973.

FIRST OF SEVEN

Nolan Ryan pitches his first no-hitter on May 15, 1973—a 3–0 victory for the Angels over the Kansas City Royals.

RYAN'S SECOND NO-NO IN THREE MONTHS
Oops! He does it again! Nolan Ryan of the Angels fires his second no-hitter, a 3–0 victory over the Tigers on July 15, 1973.

LONE STAR HERO
THE TEXAS RANGERS' JIM BIBBY NO-HITS THE OAKLAND As 6–0 ON JULY 30, 1973.

ANOTHER GEM BY BUSBY
Steve Busby of the Royals throws the second no-hitter of his career on June 19, 1974, a 2–0 victory over the Milwaukee Brewers.

BOSS MAN
Dick Bosman of the Indians throws a 4–0 no-hitter against the Oakland As on July 19, 1974.

HE'S JUST WARMING UP
September 28, 1974? Time for another Nolan Ryan no-hitter, his third. This one is a 4–0 Angels victory over the Twins.

GOING FOURTH

The incredible Nolan Ryan ties Sandy Koufax's record by pitching his fourth career no-hitter, a 1–0 Angels victory over the Orioles on June 1, 1975.

EASY ED

ED HALICKI OF THE GIANTS THROWS A NO-HITTER TO BEAT THE METS 6–0 ON AUGUST 24, 1975.

Team effort

Four Oakland As combine for a 5–0 no-hitter against the California Angels on September 28, 1975. The four are Vida Blue, Glenn Abbott, Paul Lindblad, and Rollie Fingers.

DIERKER'S GEM

Future Astros' manager Larry Dierker throws a no-hitter for the Astros on July 9, 1976, to beat the Expos 6–0.

ONE-TWO PUNCH

Johnny "Blue Moon" Odom and Francisco Barrios combine on a 2–1 no-hitter for the White Sox on July 28, 1976. The Oakland As scored on two walks, a stolen base, and an error in the fourth inning.

SWEET EFFORT BY CANDY MAN
Pittsburgh's John Candelaria no-hits the Dodgers 2–0 on August 9, 1976.

A ONE-COUNT NO-HITTER

John "The Count" Montefusco of the Giants no-hits the Braves 9–0 on September 29, 1976.

A K.C. MASTERPIECE
Jim Colborn of the Royals throws a 1–0 no-hitter against the Rangers on May 14, 1977.

Dennis the menace
Dennis Eckersley of the Cleveland Indians throws a no-hitter against the California Angels on May 30, 1977.

BEST GAME EVER PITCHED BY A GUY FROM ZEIST, HOLLAND

Rik Aalbert "Bert" Blyleven, a native of Zeist, Holland, throws a no-hitter for the Rangers to beat the Angels 6–0 on September 22, 1977.

FORSCH PLAY

On April 16, 1978, Bob Forsch of the Cardinals throws a no-hitter to beat the Phillies 5–0.

TOM TERRIFIC

Tom Seaver of the Cincinnati Reds throws his only no-hitter on June 16, 1978, beating the Cardinals 4–0.

Bouton's Back

38-year old Jim "Bulldog" Bouton, out of baseball for eight years, pitches for the Atlanta Braves and beats the Giants 4–1 on September 14, 1978.

IF HE CAN, I CAN

Bob Forsch's brother Ken throws a no-hitter for the Astros, beating the Braves 6–0 on April 7, 1979. The Forschs are the only brothers to throw no-hitters.

REUSS ROLLS

Jerry Reuss of the Los Angeles Dodgers throws a no-hitter against the Giants on June 27, 1980. Jack Clark, who reaches on an error in the first inning, was the only baserunner for the Giants.

A SIBLING MILESTONE

Phil Niekro, pitching for the Atlanta Braves, wins his 21st game of the season on September 30, 1979. On the same day, his brother Joe, pitching for the Houston Astros, wins his 21st game too.

3,000 Ks FOR STEVE CARLTON

STEVE CARLTON RECORDS CAREER STRIKEOUT #3,000 ON APRIL 29, 1981.

LIKE FATHER, LIKE SON

Umpire Paul Runge is behind the plate when Charlie Lea throws a no-hitter for the Montreal Expos on May 10, 1981, beating the San Francisco Giants.

Runge joins his father Ed as the only father-son pair to umpire at home plate for no-hitters. Ed was behind the plate on September 16, 1965, when Dave Morehead pitched a no-hitter for the Boston Red Sox.

A PERFECT NIGHT IN CLEVELAND
Len Barker of the Cleveland Indians throws a perfect game on May 15, 1981.

Another Ryan record
Nolan Ryan of the Houston Astros fires a no-hitter for the Houston Astros on September 26, 1981, his fifth, breaking a tie with Sandy Koufax for most career no-hitters. It's his only one as a National Leaguer.

HAPPY BIRTHDAY, AMERICA!
Dave Righetti throws the first Yankee no-hitter since Don Larsen's 1956 World Series perfect game on July 4, 1983, to beat the Red Sox 4–0.

A MILESTONE FOR PERRY
GAYLORD PERRY OF THE ROYALS REACHES THE 3,500 STRIKEOUT MARK ON JULY 27, 1983.

MONTREAL EXPOSED
Bob Forsch of the Cardinals throws his second no-hitter on September 26, 1983, beating the Expos 3–0.

ROOKIE GEM

Oakland's Mike Warren no-hits the White Sox 3–0 on September 29, 1983.

EARLY SEASON GEM

Jack Morris of the Detroit Tigers fires a 4–0 no-hitter against the White Sox on April 7, 1984.

FIRST A BALK THEN A PITCH

Joe Hesketh makes his major league debut with the Expos on August 7, 1984. He comes on in relief in the fifth inning, facing the Phillies in Montreal. With Jeff Stone on first, Hesketh is called for a balk before he throws his first big-league pitch.

WELL, IT'S THE LAST DAY OF THE SEASON. WHAT COULD HAPP–WAIT!

On the last day of the season, Mike Witt pitches a perfect game for the California Angels on September 30, 1984, beating the Texas Rangers 1–0.

4,000 DOWN

Danny Heep of the Mets becomes strikeout victim #4,000 for Nolan Ryan of the Houston Astros on July 11, 1985.

ROCKET SCIENCE

Roger "The Rocket" Clemens of the Boston Red Sox strikes out 20 Seattle Mariners on April 29, 1986, as the Red Sox win 3–1 in Boston.

SUPER JOE

Joe Cowley of the White Sox no-hits the Angels 7–1 on September 19, 1986. The Angels score on three walks and a sacrifice fly.

A TAXING DAY FOR JUAN NIEVES

The Brewers' Juan Nieves no-hits the Orioles 7–0 on April 15, 1987.

PERFECT!

TOM BROWNING OF THE CINCINNATI REDS THROWS A PERFECT GAME TO BEAT THE DODGERS 1–0 ON SEPTEMBER 16, 1988.

Tough way to win the pennant

Mike Scott pitches a no-hitter on September 25, 1986 to win the National League West pennant for the Houston Astros.

WHAT WAS I THINKING?

Only three people know what is said on the pitcher's mound at Shea Stadium on October 25, 1986, during the eighth inning of Game 6 of the World Series. The three are Red Sox pitcher Roger Clemens, manager John McNamara, and pitching coach Bill Fischer. Does Clemens ask to be taken out? None of the three will say. But McNamara takes Clemens out for Calvin Schiraldi. The Sox lose the game 6–5.

> ### TWO 300 GAME WINNERS IN THE SAME GAME
> *Phil Niekro and Steve Carlton both pitch for the Cleveland Indians on April 8, 1987. The teammates are both members of the 300 win club.*

WHERE DO YOU FILE YOUR NAILS—ON THE MOUND?

Pitcher Joe Niekro of the Minnesota Twins is ejected during the fourth inning of a game against the Angels when a nail file drops from his pants pocket on August 3, 1987. He is suspended for 10 games.

WHAT'S THAT IN YOUR GLOVE?

Phillies pitcher Kevin Gross is ejected in the fifth inning of a game against the Cubs on August 10, 1987 when umpires find sandpaper in his glove. He is suspended for 10 games.

Scoreless streak

Orel Hershiser IV of the Los Angeles Dodgers pitches 10 shutout innings in his last start of the season to bring his scoreless-inning streak to 59. Don Drysdale, whose record (58⅔) Hershiser breaks, broadcasts the game on September 28, 1988. The streak ends in the first inning of Hershiser's next regular season start, on April 6, 1989 when the Reds score a run.

YET ANOTHER PITCHING MILESTONE
Nolan Ryan strikes out his 5,000th victim, Rickey Henderson, on August 28, 1989.

A TWO-MAN NO-HITTER
Mark Langston and Mike Witt of the Angels combine on a no-hitter to beat the Mariners 1–0 on April 11, 1990.

BIG ONE FOR BIG UNIT

The Mariners' Randy Johnson pitches his first career no-hitter, beating the Tigers 2–0 on June 2, 1990.

RYAN'S EXPRESS ROLES ON
Nolan Ryan of the Texas Rangers pitches his sixth no-hitter on June 11, 1990.

TWO IN ONE LINE

Dave Stewart of the Oakland As in the American League throws a no-hitter against the Toronto Blue Jays on June 29, 1990.

And in the National League, Fernando Valenzuela of the Los Angeles Dodgers throws a no-hitter against the St. Louis Cardinals—the only day in modern big league history to see two no-hitters.

300 FOR RYAN

NOLAN RYAN OF THE TEXAS RANGERS WINS HIS 300TH GAME, ON JULY 30, 1990.

MULHOLLAND DRIVE

Terry Mulholland of the Phillies fires a 6–0 no-hitter to beat the Giants on August 15, 1990.

DAVE STIEB'S NO-HITTER

Dave Stieb fires a 3–0 no-hitter for the Blue Jays on September 2, 1990.

A NEW STANDARD

Bobby Thigpen of the Chicago White Sox becomes first pitcher to record 50 saves in a season on September 15, 1990. He finishes the season with 57 saves.

WHIFF, WHIFF, WHIFF

Nolan Ryan of the Texas Rangers strikes out 17 on May 1, 1991 and beats the Blue Jays 3–0 in Toronto on his way to a victory in the record seventh and final no-hitter of his career.

GREENE DAY

The Phillies' Tommy Greene pitches a 2–0 no-hitter to beat the Expos on May 23, 1991.

DOES NOT PLAY WELL WITH OTHERS

Reds pitcher Rob Dibble, one of the "Nasty Boys," throws a ball into the left field bleachers in Cincinnati and hits teacher Meg Porter. He is suspended for four games, April 21, 1991.

A COMBINED EFFORT

Bob Milacki, Mike Flanagan, Mark Williamson, and Gregg Olson of the Baltimore Orioles combine on a 2–0 no-hitter against the Oakland As on July 13, 1991.

A GEM FOR DENNIS MARTINEZ

On July 28, 1991, Dennis Martinez of the Montreal Expos throws a perfect game to beat the Los Angeles Dodgers 2–0.

WAY TO GO, KID

Wilson Alvarez of the Chicago White Sox throws a no-hitter against the Baltimore Orioles in his second big league start, and his first for the White Sox on August 11, 1991.

ROYAL TREATMENT
Bret Saberhagen of the Kansas City Royals no-hits the White Sox on August 26, 1991.

THREE-MAN GEM
Three Atlanta Braves pitchers—Kent Mercker, Mark Wohlers, and Alejandro Pena—combine to pitch a 1–0 no-hitter against the Padres on September 1, 1991.

THAT'S GROSS!
KEVIN GROSS OF THE DODGERS NO-HITS THE GIANTS 2–0 ON AUGUST 17, 1992.

Hitless in Seattle
Chris Bosio of the Mariners no-hits the Red Sox at the Kingdome on April 22, 1993.

YOUR ATTENTION PLEASE: NOW PITCHING, JOSÉ CANSECO
Slugging Texas Rangers outfielder José Canseco pitches the eighth inning against the Red Sox on May 29, 1993 and tears ligaments in his arm. He needs surgery and is out for the rest of the season.

KRUK V. JOHNSON

In the 1993 All-Star Game in Baltimore on July 14, Randy Johnson of the American League pitches to John Kruk of the National. Kruk ducks and backs out—laughing and shaking his head—making it clear that he wants no part of Johnson.

AN INCREDIBLE ACHIEVEMENT

Jim Abbott of the New York Yankees, born without a right hand, pitches a no-hitter on September 4, 1993, and beats the Cleveland Indians 4–0.

DARRYL! DARRYL!

Darryl Kile of the Houston Astros fires a no-hitter against the Mets on September 8, 1993.

A NICE ROUND NUMBER LIKE 5,714

Nolan Ryan of the Texas Rangers records the final strikeout of his career on September 16, 1993—#5,714. The victim is Greg Myers of the Angels.

All by himself

Kent Mercker's first no-hitter was part of a combined one on September 11, 1991. But on April 8, 1994, he pitches a no-hitter all by himself for the Braves to beat the Dodgers 6–0.

GREAT SCOTT

The Twins' Scott Erickson fires a 6–0 no-hitter against the Brewers on April 27, 1994.

Perfect Angels

Kenny Rogers of the Texas Rangers throws a perfect game—the first lefty to do so in the American League—on July 28, 1994, defeating the Angels 4–0.

WOW!

Robb Nen of the Marlins faces Dave Otto of the Cubs—the first time pitchers with palindromic names have ever faced each other—on August 3, 1994. Marlins 9, Cubs 8.

PERFECT BUT NOT OFFICIAL

Pedro Martinez of the Montreal Expos pitches nine perfect innings against the Padres in San Diego on June 3, 1995. But the Expos can't score, and the game goes into extra innings. In the tenth, Martinez allows a double by Bip Roberts and is lifted for Mel Rojas, who closes out the Expos' 1–0 victory.

BIG BROTHER

The Dodgers' Ramon Martinez, Pedro's brother (see above) no-hits the Florida Marlins on July 14, 1995.

THE BASEBALL GEEK'S BIBLE

Dr. No

Dwight "Dr. K" Gooden of the New York Yankees throws a 2–0 no-hitter to beat the Mariners on May 14, 1996.

20-20 CLUB

Roger Clemens matches his feat of 10 years ago by striking out 20 Detroit Tigers in Boston on September 18, 1996.

LEITER FLUID

Alois "Al" Leiter of the Florida Marlins fires a no-hitter to beat the Rockies 11–0 on May 11, 1996.

A NO-NO FOR NOMO

Hideo Nomo of the Dodgers pitches his first no-hitter, a 9–0 victory over the Rockies in Denver on September 17, 1996.

Giant killer

Kevin Brown of the Florida Marlins no-hits the Giants on June 10, 1997.

LOTS OF Ks FOR RANDY JOHNSON
6'10" Randy Johnson of the Seattle Mariners strikes
out 19 Oakland Athletics on June 24, 1997.

ASTRO-NOTS
Francisco Cordova of the Pirates pitches nine innings,
and Ricardo Rincon one for the Pirates to no-hit the
Astros on July 12, 1997.

Wood strikes out his age
20-year-old Kerry Wood of the Chicago Cubs
strikes out his age, fanning 20 Houston Astros
on May 6, 1998.

WELLS DONE
DAVID WELLS OF THE NEW YORK YANKEES THROWS
A PERFECT GAME ON MAY 17, 1998.

CLEMENS FANS #3,000
Roger Clemens of the Toronto Blue Jays strikes
out Randy Winn of the Tampa Bay Devil Rays for
the 3,000th strikeout of his career, July 5, 1998.

JOSÉ VS. RANDY

José Jimenez of the Cardinals throws a 1–0 no-hitter in Phoenix to beat Randy Johnson of the Diamondbacks on June 25, 1999. Johnson strikes out 13 in the losing effort, including his 2,500th victim.

YOGI MAGIC

It's July 18, 1999, "Yogi Berra Day" at Yankee Stadium. Don Larsen, who pitched a perfect game in the 1956 World Series, throws out the ceremonial first pitch to his catcher, Hall of Famer Yogi Berra. Berra borrows Joe Girardi's catcher's mitt for the ceremony, then returns it. He leaves some Yogi magic in the glove, because in the subsequent game, David Cone is perfect against the Montreal Expos, winning 6–0. Even though Cone had pitched in the National League, none of the Expos batters had ever faced Cone before.

ERIC THE GREAT

On September 11, 1999, Eric Milton of the Twins pitches a 7–0 no hitter against the Angels.

I LOST COUNT AT 589

Opening Day: Roger Clemens of the New York Yankees passes Walter Johnson as the all-time strikeout leader in the American League on April 2, 2001, by striking out Joe Randa of the Kansas City Royals, the 3,509th career strikeout for Clemens. Clemens breaks that record another 590 times (maybe that's a record, too!) through the end of his career in the American League. In 2004, Clemens signs with the Astros.

NOMO'S NO-NO #2

Hideo Nomo of the Boston Red Sox pitches a no-hitter—his second—on April 4, 2001, to beat the Orioles 3–0.

ANOTHER RANDY DANDY

Randy Johnson of the Arizona Diamondbacks strikes out 20 Reds in 11 innings on May 8, 2001. Johnson does not tie the nine-inning record because the game goes 11 innings, although he strikes out 20 in the first 9 innings.

A great day for A. J.

A.J. Burnett of the Marlins no-hits the Padres 3–0 on May 12, 2001.

HEY, BUD
Bud Smith of the Cardinals no-hits the Padres on September 3, 2001.

THE LOWE-DOWN
BOSTON'S DEREK LOWE NO-HITS THE TAMPA BAY DEVIL RAYS 10–0 ON APRIL 27, 2002.

An inauspicious debut
J.J. Trujillo makes his major league debut as a pitcher for the San Diego Padres on June 11, 2002. In an interleague game, the first batter he faces is Tony Batista of the Baltimore Orioles in the bottom of the ninth inning with the score tied at 5. Batista homers and Trujillo becomes the first pitcher to surrender a walk-off home run to the first batter he faces in the major leagues.

IT DOESN'T MATTER WHO WINS. IT'S THE TAKING PART THAT COUNTS!
The annual All-Star Game ends in a 7–7 tie on July 9, 2002 at Miller Park in Milwaukee as both teams run out of pitchers.

TEAMMATES TRIUMPH

On September 16, 2002, Curt Schilling and Randy Johnson of the Arizona Diamondbacks do something which no teammates have ever done before: They both strike out 300 in the same season.

> *GIANTS PUT THROUGH THE MILL*
> *Kevin Millwood of the Phillies throws a no-hitter on April 27, 2003 to beat the Giants 1–0.*

THE JOY OF SIX

Using a record six pitchers, the Houston Astros combine on a no-hitter against the New York Yankees on June 11, 2003. The Astros pitchers are Roy Oswalt, Pete Munro, Kirk Saarloos, Brad Lidge, Octavio Dotel, and Billy Wagner. Prior to this game, the Yankees had hits in 6,980 consecutive games dating back to 1958.

ONE GAME, TWO MILESTONES
Roger Clemens of the New York Yankees reaches two milestones in the same game on June 13, 2003. In striking out Edgar Renteria of the St. Louis Cardinals, Clemens notches career strikeout #4,000, and Clemens's win is the 300th of his career.

PERFECT UNIT

Randy Johnson of the Arizona Diamondbacks throws his second no-hitter, and it's a perfect game on May 18, 2004. The game is Johnson's first no-hitter since June 2, 1990. The 14-year gap between no-hitters is a record.

THAT'S A LOT OF STRIKEOUTS!

Randy Johnson of the Arizona Diamondbacks notches career strikeout #4,000 on June 29, 2004 when he fans Jeff Cirillo of the San Diego Padres.

A HOMETOWN ALL-STAR

Roger Clemens signs with the Houston Astros before the start of the 2004 season, so he can be close to his family in Houston. On July 13, 2004, he is the starting pitcher for the National League in the All-Star Game, played in Houston. At 41, Clemens is the oldest man ever to start an All-Star Game. He pitches dreadfully, gives up six runs, and is the losing pitcher.

The World Series

"The best possible thing in baseball is winning the World Series. The second best thing is losing the World Series."

Tommy Lasorda

WHERE THE WORLD BEGAN

The first game of the modern World Series is played at the Huntington Avenue Grounds in Boston on October 1, 1903. The Pirates beat the Pilgrims 7–3 before a crowd of 16,242.

THREE FOR BIG SIX

In one of the most overpowering performances in the history of the World Series, Christy Mathewson of the New York Giants shuts out the Philadelphia As for the third time in Game 5 as the Giants win the game 2–0 and the series 4–1 on October 14, 1905.

THE HITLESS WONDERS

The Chicago White Sox, who batted just .230 during the regular season, beat the Cubs in Game 6 on October 14, 1906 to win the Series 4–2.

HEY, BLUE!

Game 1 of the 1909 World Series played on October 8 between the Pittsburgh Pirates and the Detroit Tigers at Forbes Field in Pittsburgh is the first to use four umpires.

YOU ARE OUT!

Frank Chance of the Chicago Cubs is the first player ever ejected from a World Series on October 20, 1910 in Game 3. He argues with future Hall of Fame umpire Tom Connolly.

AN INFAMOUS ERROR

1912 World Series, Game 8, New York Giants vs. Boston Red Sox in Boston on October 16. (Game 2 had ended in a tie.) In the bottom of the tenth inning with the Giants ahead 3–2, Clyde Engle, pinch hitting for pitcher "Smokey" Joe Wood, lofts a soft fly ball to center field. Fred Snodgrass drops it. Although there are other misplays in the inning, "The Snodgrass Muff" haunts him for the rest of his life. The Red Sox win the game 3–2 and take the Series 4–3–1.

THE MIRACLE BRAVES SWEEP THE SERIES

The "Miracle Braves," in last place in the middle of July, come back to win the National League pennant by 10½ games and sweep the Philadelphia Athletics in the World Series on October 13, 1914—the first four-game Series sweep.

WILD ABOUT HARRY

Harry Hooper of the Boston Red Sox becomes the first man to hit two home runs in a World Series game (Game 5) on October 13, 1915.

Sibling rivalry

Wheeler "Doc" Johnston of the Cleveland Indians and his brother Jimmy of the Brooklyn Dodgers become the first brothers to face each other in the World Series on October 6, 1920 in Game 2. The Indians win the best of nine Series 5–2.

I'D RATHER DO IT MYSELF!

Indians second baseman Bill Wambsganss turns an unassisted triple play on October 10, 1920 in the fifth inning of Game 5 of the World Series—one of the greatest moments in baseball history.

RADIO DAYS

The first World Series game to be broadcast on radio is Game 1 of the 1921 Series between the New York Yankees and the New York Giants October 5. All eight (best of nine) games are played at the stadium they shared, the Polo Grounds.

COOLIDGE IS NUMBER ONE IN MY BOOK
Calvin Coolidge is the first president to see the first game of a World Series. The Giants beat the Senators 4–3 at Griffith Stadium in Washington, D.C. on October 4, 1924.

YOUNGEST MANAGER TO WIN THE SERIES
Bucky Harris is named to manage the 1924 Washington Senators. Under his leadership, the Senators take the American League pennant and win the World Series in 1924. They are pennant-winners again in 1925.

LOOK OUT!
In the top of the eighth inning of the final game of the 1924 World Series between the Washington Senators and the New York Giants on October 10, the Giants are ahead 3–1 with the bases loaded when player-manager Bucky Harris of the Senators hits a hard grounder to third. The ball hits a pebble and bounces over Fred Lindstrom's head and into left field. Two runs score to tie the game. In the 12th inning, Muddy Ruel of the Senators hits a pop foul near home plate. Giants catcher Hank Gowdy steps on his discarded mask and can't get his foot out. No catch. Given an extra life, Ruel doubles. Walter Johnson reaches on an error and Earl McNeely hits a sharp grounder to Fred Lindstrom. Once again, the ball bounces over his head. Ruel scores. Ballgame over. The Washington Senators are World Champions.

Did Rice catch it?

On October 10, 1925 in Game 3 of the World Series, Earl Smith of the Pittsburgh Pirates hits a long drive to right center field. Sam Rice, with the Washington Senators, makes what seems to be a spectacular backhand stab for the ball, and falls into the stands. When he gets up, he has the ball in his glove. Umpire Cy Rigler rules "catch," and Smith is out. The Pirates protest but lose. Washington wins the game 4–3, and the Series 4–3. But some people question whether Rice actually caught the ball. Rice refused to say, but left a letter to be opened after his death. The letter, opened at the Hall of Fame, said "I had a death grip on it. At no time did I lose possession of the ball."

THREE FOR THE BAMBINO

In Game 4 of the Yankees–Cardinals World Series, on October 6, 1926, Babe Ruth hits three home runs to lead the Yankees to a 10–5 victory at Sportsman's Park.

ALEXANDER THE GREAT

Leading 3–2 in the seventh inning of Game 7 of the World Series on October 10, 1926, Cardinal pitcher Jesse Haines develops a blister on his pitching hand. Grover Cleveland Alexander comes in from the bullpen to pitch. He was probably hung over or had been sleeping in the bullpen (he had pitched in Game 6). The Yankees have the bases loaded with Tony Lazzeri at the plate. Alexander strikes out Lazzeri on four pitches to end the inning.

THAT'S IT? THE SERIES IS OVER? WHAT HAPPENED?

Babe Ruth homers in the third inning of Game 7 of the 1926 Cardinals–Yankees World Series in New York on October 10. In the bottom of the ninth, with the Cardinals ahead 3–2, Ruth is on first base with two outs. On his own, Ruth inexplicably tries to steal second but is thrown out by Cardinals catcher Bob O'Farrell for the final out of the inning, the game, and the Series. The Cardinals win the Series 4–3.

A WILD FINISH

The mighty 1927 New York Yankees, considered one of the greatest teams ever, beat the Pittsburgh Pirates in Game 4 of the World Series on October 8 because of a wild pitch. The game is tied at three in the ninth inning with the bases loaded with Yankees. Pirates pitcher Johnny Miljus strikes out Lou Gehrig and Bob Meusel. He takes Tony Lazzeri to a two-strike count, then uncorks his second wild pitch of the inning. Earle Combs scores, ball game over, World Series over. Yankees sweep the Pirates 4–0.

BABE STRIKES TWICE

For the second time in his career, Babe Ruth hits two home runs in a World Series game on October 9, 1928 as the Yankees beat the Cardinals 7–3 in Game 4 and sweep the Series 4–0.

HE'S GOING TO PITCH IN THE WORLD SERIES?

In the first game of the 1929 World Series on October 8, the surprise starting pitcher for the Philadelphia Athletics is 35-year-old Howard Ehmke, who won only seven games during the regular season. But manager Connie Mack's strategy works, as Ehmke strikes out 13 Cubs at Wrigley Field and, in his final major league win, leads the As to a 3–1 victory. The As go on to win the Series 4–1.

THE CALLED SHOT

During the fifth inning of Game 3 of the World Series at Chicago's Wrigley Field on October 1, 1932, Babe Ruth steps out of the batter's box and gestures towards left field—then hits a home run right there—the "called shot." The Yankees win the game 7–5 and sweep the Cubs 4–0.

> ### DUCK, DUCKY!
> *In Game 7 of the 1934 World Series, played in Detroit on October 9, the Tigers fans are irate at Joe "Ducky" Medwick of the St. Louis Cardinals for a hard slide into the Tigers' Marv Owen at third base in the top of the sixth inning. Medwick and Owen fight briefly without injury. But the Detroit fans shower garbage and debris on Medwick in left field, and in the bottom of the sixth, Commissioner Kenesaw Mountain Landis orders Medwick to be removed from the game for his own safety. The Cardinals win the game 11–0.*

LAST OF A BREED

The World Series of 1934 was the last with two player-managers. Second baseman/manager Frankie Frisch of the Cardinals faces catcher/manager Mickey Cochrane of the Detroit Tigers, with the Cardinals prevailing four games to three.

LOMBARDI'S SNOOZE

One of the most memorable plays in the history of the Series happens in the fourth game of the 1939 World Series between the Cincinnati Reds and the New York Yankees. On October 8, in the top of the tenth inning, with the game tied at 4, Joe DiMaggio singles. Rightfielder Ival Goodman misplays the ball and Frank Crosetti scores. As Charlie Keller scores, he bowls over Reds catcher Ernie Lombardi and the ball rolls away. While Lombardi lays there dazed, DiMaggio scores. The Yankees win the game 7–4 and sweep the Series 4–0.

THE DROPPED THIRD STRIKE

The Dodgers lead the New York Yankees 4–3 with two outs in the top of the ninth inning of Game 4 of the 1941 World Series on October 5. Hugh Casey pitches to Tommy Henrich with nobody on. A Brooklyn win ties the series at two. Henrich swings at a 3–2 pitch and misses, but Dodger catcher Mickey Owen misses the ball. As it rolls to the Dodger dugout, Henrich runs to first. Passed ball. The inning continues and Joe DiMaggio comes to bat. He singles and Charlie Keller doubles, driving in Henrich and DiMaggio. Keller and Bill Dickey also score, and the Yankees win 7–4. They go on to win the Series 4–1.

A BATTERY OF BROTHERS
Mort and Walker Cooper of the St. Louis Cardinals become the first brother pitcher-catcher pair in the World Series, Game 1, September 30, 1942. They team up together again in the Series of 1943 and '44.

SLAUGHTER'S MAD DASH
In the eighth inning of Game 7 of the 1946 World Series between the Cardinals and Red Sox, Enos "Country" Slaughter singles. Then, with two outs, he breaks for second when Harry "The Hat" Walker doubles into the left centerfield gap. Slaughter keeps running. The throw is not quite in time, and Slaughter scores to put the Cardinals ahead. His non-stop trip from first base home becomes known as "Slaughter's mad dash." The Cardinals win both the game and the Series.

Six umps in the series
The first game of the 1947 Series between the Dodgers and the Yankees on September 30 is the first to use six umpires.

PINCH ME!
Yogi Berra of the New York Yankees hits the first pinch-hit home run in Series history, off Ralph Branca of the Brooklyn Dodgers on October 2, 1947 during Game 3. The Yankees lose the game 9–8 but win the Series 4–3.

SO NEAR AND YET...

Bill Bevens of the Yankees pitches a no-hit ball into the ninth inning on October 3, 1947 in Game 4 of the World Series, but pinch hitter Cookie Lavagetto of the Brooklyn Dodgers doubles with two outs and the Dodgers win the game 3–2. The Yankees still win the Series 4–3.

A MEMORABLE CATCH BY AL GIONFRIDDO

In Game 6 of the 1947 Series on October 5, before a record crowd of over 74,000 at Yankee Stadium, Joe DiMaggio of the Yankees hits a ball 415 feet to left field. 5'6" Al Gionfriddo of the Dodgers, playing in his final major league game, makes a phenomenal catch to deprive DiMaggio of a home run. Brooklyn wins the game 8–6, but the Yankees win Game 7 and the Series.

> ### THE MOST FAMOUS NONPICK-OFF IN THE HISTORY OF THE WORLD SERIES
>
> *In Game 1 of the 1948 Series between the Cleveland Indians and the Boston Braves, on October 6, Boston's Phil Masi is on second base in the bottom of the eighth inning. Bob Feller fires to Joe Gordon at second base in an attempt to pick Masi off the bag. But umpire Bill Stewart calls Masi safe. Indians manager Lou Boudreau argues in vain to get Stewart to change the call. The call stands, and Masi goes on to score the only run of the game. Cleveland takes the Series anyway, 4–1.*

DOWN THE DRAIN

In Game 2 of the 1951 World Series between the Yankees and the Giants on October 5, Yankee right fielder Mickey Mantle steps in a drain cover in the fifth inning and severely injures his right knee. He's out for the rest of the Series (which the Yankees win 4–2.) Knee and leg problems plague Mantle for the rest of his career.

And it's not even soccer!

One of the most controversial plays in World Series history happens during the fifth inning of Game 3 of the 1951 Giants–Yankees World Series on October 8. Eddie Stanky of the Giants is on first base and tries to steal second. The throw comes in to Yankee shortstop Phil Rizzuto, covering second base. Rizzuto tags Stanky, but Stanky kicks the ball out of Rizzuto's glove and goes on to third. The Giants win the game 6–2, but the Yankees win the Series 4–2.

MARTIN'S HEADS-UP PLAY

Second baseman Billy Martin's catch saves the game and the Series for the New York Yankees in Game 7 of the 1952 World Series on October 7 against the Dodgers at Ebbets Field in Brooklyn. Jackie Robinson comes to bat in the bottom of the seventh with the Yankees ahead 4–2 and the bases "FOB"—Full Of Brooklyns. Robinson hits a little blooper in the infield and it looks ready to drop for a hit as the other infielders freeze. Martin makes a running knee-high catch to save the game and the championship for the Yankees, who win the game 4–2 and the Series 4–3.

> ### *"THE CATCH"*
> *At the base of the right center field wall at the Polo Grounds in New York, Willie Mays of the New York Giants makes an over-the-shoulder catch of a blast by Vic Wertz of the Cleveland Indians in Game 1 of the World Series on September 29, 1954—considered such a great catch that it is known as "THE catch." Then he turns and fires to second base to keep the runner on first from tagging up.*

YOGI STILL THINKS HE WAS OUT

In Game 1 of the Dodgers–Yankees World Series of 1955, Jackie Robinson of the Dodgers steals home in the eighth inning on September 28, 1955. Home plate umpire Bill Summers calls him safe. Yankee catcher Yogi Berra insists he made the tag in time. Yogi still thinks so.

THE BASEBALL GEEK'S BIBLE

Amoros saves the day

The Brooklyn Dodgers had played the New York Yankees in the World Series in 1947, 1949, 1952, and 1953, and lost each time. In 1955, the Dodgers take the Yankees to Game 7 on October 4 at Yankee Stadium. Johnny Podres is pitching a 2–0 shutout for Brooklyn when Yogi Berra comes to bat with two men on in the bottom of the sixth inning. Berra, a lefty batter, hits a drive to the 301 foot sign by the left field foul pole. Left fielder Sandy Amoros runs almost to the wall, and puts out his glove as far as he can to make the catch. Then he throws to Pee Wee Reese at shortstop who fires to Gil Hodges to double Gil McDougald off first base. Instead of a 2–2 tie with no outs and the go-ahead run on second, it's still 2–0 with two outs and a runner on second. Podres holds on to win the game and the Brooklyn Dodgers win their only World Series 4–3. The Dodgers no longer have to hear "Wait 'til next year!"

PERFECT!

Don Larsen of the New York Yankees pitches a perfect game and beats the Brooklyn Dodgers 2–0 in Game 5 of the World Series on October 8, 1956—the single greatest one-game performance in the history of the sport.

WHERE DID I LEAVE MY CAR?

The largest crowd ever to see a World Series game—92,706—watches the Los Angeles Dodgers play the Chicago White Sox in Game 5 at the Los Angeles Coliseum on October 6, 1959. The Dodgers are playing at the Coliseum because their new stadium, Dodger Stadium, won't open until 1962. The Sox win the game 1–0. The attendance at the Coliseum is more than twice the largest attendance at Chicago's Comiskey Park. The Dodgers win the Series 4–2.

THE PIRATES WIN THE SERIES! THE PIRATES WIN THE SERIES!

The Pittsburgh Pirates beat the New York Yankees 10–9 to win the World Series four games to three on October 13, 1960 when Bill Mazeroski hits a home run in the bottom of the ninth inning at Forbes Field. Yankees second baseman Bobby Richardson (.367 with 12 RBIs) is named the Series' MVP even though his team loses—a unique achievement. The Yankees outscored the Pirates 55–27. This is the first time that a World Series is decided by a home run in the bottom of the ninth inning of the seventh game.

AN INCREDIBLE RECORD FOR THE INCREDIBLE WHITEY FORD

New York City native Edward "Whitey" Ford pitches 33⅔ scoreless innings in the World Series. The streak spans three Series—1960 (18 innings), 1961 (14), and 1962 (1⅔). Very few men get to pitch 33⅔ innings in the Series. The streak lasts from a complete game 10–0 victory in Game 3 of the 1960 World Series until Willie Mays scores with two outs in the bottom of the second inning of the first game of the 1962 Series against the Giants.

A dramatic end

The World Championship is on the line on October 16, 1962 in the seventh game of the Yankees–Giants World Series at Candlestick Park. The Giants are behind 1–0 but have runners at second and third with two outs in the bottom of the ninth inning. Willie McCovey lines a pitch from Ralph Terry right into second baseman Bobby Richardson's glove. Game over. Series over. Yankees win!

A NEW STRIKEOUT RECORD
Sandy Koufax of the Los Angeles Dodgers strikes out a World Series record 15 Yankees on October 2, 1963 in Game 1.

OH, BROTHER!
On October 15, 1964, Ken and Clete Boyer become the first brothers to homer in the same World Series game. Clete homers for the Yankees and Ken for the Cardinals as St. Louis wins the seventh game 7–5 and the Series 4–3.

HEY, THE RED SOX WERE IN THE SERIES!
Former Ambassador Joseph Kennedy is at Fenway Park to watch the Boston Red Sox host the St. Louis Cardinals in Game 1 of the World Series on October 4, 1967. After a fainting spell, his sons, Senators Robert and Edward, help their father to his car, *then go back to the game*.

A NEWER STRIKEOUT RECORD
Bob Gibson of the St. Louis Cardinals strikes out a record 17 Tigers on October 2 in Game 1 of the 1968 World Series.

HIS FIRST HOMER IS IN THE WORLD SERIES

Ever wonder whether professional ballplayers get worked up when they appear in the World Series? On October 3, 1968, in Game 2 of the Series against the Cardinals, Tigers pitcher Mickey Lolich comes to bat in the third inning, and hits the first home run of his career.

WHEN SOMEBODY'S "VERSION" OF THE NATIONAL ANTHEM BECOMES AN ISSUE

On October 7, 1968, at Tiger Stadium in Detroit, José Feliciano sings a non-traditional version of the Star Spangled Banner before Game 5 of the World Series. The controversy over his soulful rendition of the anthem almost overshadows the Series.

ONE OF THE GREATEST CATCHES EVER

Ron Swoboda of the Mets makes a great diving catch in right center field on October 15 on a ninth-inning Brooks Robinson drive with two men on to help New York beat the Baltimore Orioles in Game 4 of the 1969 World Series.

EARL WEAVER, THIS THUMB'S FOR YOU

Baltimore Orioles' manager Earl Weaver is ejected from Game 4 of the 1969 World Series on October 15 by umpire Shag Crawford.

SHOE POLISH!

The seven-year-old "Miracle Mets" beat the heavily favored Baltimore Orioles 5–3 in Game 5 to win the World Series on October 16, 1969. During the sixth inning, Cleon Jones claims that a pitch hit him on the shoe. Mets manager Gil Hodges shows umpire Lou DiMuro what he claims is shoe polish on the ball, and Jones is awarded first base. The next batter, future lawyer Donn Clendenon homers. The Mets win the game 5–3 and the Series 4–1.

The human vacuum cleaner

Just as streaks (DiMaggio's, Ripken's, Rose's) sometimes collectively count as "moments" so too must Brooks Robinson's brilliant run- and game-saving play at third base for the Baltimore Orioles during the 1970 World Series against the Cincinnati Reds from October 10–15. Robinson is named the MVP of the Series, which Baltimore won 4–1.

FAKING IT

For the first time, a World Series game is played on a surface which is not called "grass." Game 1 at Cincinnati on October 10, 1970, featuring the Orioles and the Reds, is played on Riverfront Stadium's artificial turf.

A MISSED CALL BY AN UMPIRE WHO MISSED THE PLAY

In 1970, the first World Series game played on artificial surface also sees one of the worst and most controversial calls in history. In the sixth inning, Ty Cline of the Reds hits a nubber towards the pitcher. Orioles catcher Elrod Hendricks fields the ball and slaps a tag with his left hand on Bernie Carbo of the Reds as he slides home. Home plate umpire Ken Burkhart, who is upended on the play and has his back to the tag, calls Carbo out. But Hendricks was holding the ball in his right hand. Burkhart clearly got it wrong. Baltimore wins the game 4–3 and the Series 4–1.

Self support

In Game 3 of the 1970 World Series on October 13, pitcher Dave McNally of the Baltimore Orioles becomes the first pitcher ever to hit a grand slam in the World Series.

TONIGHT'S THE NIGHT

The Pittsburgh Pirates beat the Baltimore Orioles at home in Game 4 of the World Series on October 13, 1971—the first World Series game at night.

GREATEST FAKE-OUT IN BASEBALL HISTORY

It's Game 3 of the World Series, October 18, 1972. Joe Morgan is on second and Bobby Tolan on third for the Cincinnati Reds. Rollie Fingers is on the mound for the Oakland Athletics. Johnny Bench of the Reds batting in the eighth inning with a 3–2 count. The As manager Dick Williams walks to the mound to talk with Fingers. Williams gestures to first base, which is unoccupied. After Williams goes back to the dugout, Oakland catcher Gene Tenace sticks his right hand out to signal for an intentional walk. But Fingers's next pitch is a strike down the middle—taking Bench completely by surprise. Bench is out (not to mention embarrassed) and the inning is over. But the Reds win the game 1–0.

YOU'RE FIRED

Livid because Mike Andrews of the Oakland Athletics made two errors in the 12th inning of Game 2 of the 1973 World Series against the New York Mets on October 14, team owner Charles O. Finley tries to cut Andrews from the team, claiming that he was "injured." Baseball commissioner Bowie Kuhn barred the move.

THINK HE WAS UP FOR THE GAME?

Because the Oakland As are in the American League, which uses the designated hitter, pitcher Ken Holtzman has not come to bat during the 1974 season or the American League Championship Series. But the World Series against the Los Angeles Dodgers is played by National League rules—no DH.

So Holtzman comes to bat in Game 4 of the Series on October 16, 1974 and homers in the third inning off Andy Messersmith. The As win the game 5–2, and the Series 4–1.

No interference

In the bottom of the tenth inning of Game 3 of the 1975 World Series on October 10, with the game tied at 5, and a runner on first, Ed Armbrister of the Reds bunts, but is slow leaving the batter's box. Red Sox catcher Carlton Fisk fields the ball but makes an errant throw to second base and the ball goes into the outfield. Fisk claims that Armbrister interfered with his throw. Home plate umpire Larry Barnett rules that there was no interference. Error on Fisk. The Reds win the game 6–5 and the Series 4–3.

THE BODY ENGLISH HOME RUN

In the 12th inning of Game 6 of the 1975 Reds–Red Sox World Series, on October 21, Carlton Fisk of the Red Sox hits a home run—or was it just a long foul ball? After hitting it, Fisk does everything he can to wave the ball fair—and so it is. The Sox win 7–6. But it isn't enough, as the Reds win Game 7.

IT'S NOT CCCCCCOLD!

It's 43° at game time on October 17, 1976—the first Sunday night game in World Series history. Seated in a field level box at Cincinnati's Riverfront Stadium without a hat, coat, or gloves, is commissioner Bowie Kuhn. The Reds beat the Yankees 4–3, and go on to sweep the Series 4–0.

WELL DESERVED

Reggie Jackson proves that he deserves the nickname "Mr. October" on October 18, 1977 by hitting home runs off three different Los Angeles pitchers—each on the first pitch—in Game 6 to win the World Series for New York. And because he had homered in his final at-bat in Game 5, Jackson's feat is four consecutive World Series home runs.

THAT'S USING YOUR HIP!

Reggie Jackson of the New York Yankees is on first base and Thurman Munson is on second with one out in the sixth inning of Game 4 of the 1978 World Series on October 14. Lou Piniella hits a ball which hits Dodger shortstop Bill Russell's glove. Thurman Munson runs towards third. Russell steps on second to force Jackson, then throws to Steve Garvey at first for a double play. But the ball never gets there, because it hits Jackson's right hip and rolls into right field. Munson scores. Although the Dodgers claim that Jackson intentionally interfered and that Piniella should therefore be called out, no interference call is made and the run counts. The Yankees win the game in 10 innings 4–3, and win the Series 4–2.

A two-man catch

During the ninth inning of the sixth and final game of the 1980 World Series on October 28, Frank White of the Kansas City Royals hits a pop foul by the first base dugout. The ball pops out of Phillies' catcher Bob Boone's mitt, right into the glove of Pete Rose, who is backing up on the play. Out! The Phillies win the game 4–1 and the Series 4–2.

HIGH FIVE!

Paul Molitor of the Milwaukee Brewers becomes the first man to get five hits in one World Series game on October 12, 1982, Game 1 of the Series against the Cardinals.

SOMETHING BREWING

Robin Yount has four hits in each of two games of the 1982 World Series for the Milwaukee Brewers—the first man to accomplish this unusual feat. He has three singles and a double in Game 1 on October 12, followed by a homer, a single, and a double on October 17 in Game 5.

Hall of famer George Anderson

When the Detroit Tigers win the World Series in 1984, it marks the first time that a manager— George "Sparky" Anderson—wins the World Championship with teams in both leagues. He also won with the 1975 and 1976 Cincinnati Reds, "The Big Red Machine!"

OOPS!

The 1986 World Series matches the New York Mets against the Boston Red Sox, who have not won the Series since 1918. On October 25, in Game 6, the Sox are one strike away from a Series victory—in the bottom of the tenth inning, when the Shea Stadium scoreboard prematurely and, as it turns out inaccurately, flashes "CONGRATULATIONS BOSTON RED SOX, 1986 WORLD SERIES WINNERS." New York wins the game when Mookie Wilson's dribbler up the first base line goes through Bill Buckner's legs. The Mets then put the deflated Sox away in Game 7 to win the Series.

AN UNLIKELY HOME RUN

Utility infielder Tom Lawless of the St. Louis Cardinals hits a home run in Game 4 of the 1987 World Series for the St. Louis Cardinals off Joe Niekro of the Minnesota Twins. It's his first home run of the 1987 season. The Cardinals win 7–2, but the Twins win the Series 4–3.

UNBELIEVABLE

Kirk Gibson of the Los Angeles Dodgers, hobbled by bad legs, hits a bottom-of-the-ninth, game-winning pinch-hit two-run homer off Dennis Eckersley of the Oakland Athletics on October 15 to win Game 1 of the 1988 World Series. Broadcaster Jack Buck captures the sentiment of millions of fans: "I don't believe what I just saw!" The Dodgers go on to win the Series 4–1.

THE MOST IMPORTANT WORDS IN BASEBALL: PAY ATTENTION!

In the eighth inning of Game 7 of the 1991 World Series, the Twins and Braves battle in a scoreless tie. Lonnie Smith of the Braves is on first when Terry Pendleton doubles. Smith apparently loses sight of the ball for a moment, and Twins second baseman Chuck Knoblauch dekes him into thinking that he had the ball. Smith stops at third and never scores. Jack Morris goes the distance for a complete game— 10-inning, 1–0 win for the Twins on October 27, 1991 at the Metrodome in Minneapolis.

¡SdOO

At the start of Game 2 of the 1992 World Series between the Toronto Blue Jays and the Braves in Atlanta, the U.S. Marine Corps Color Guard carries an inverted Canadian flag by mistake.

THE FIRST STEP IN A TRULY WORLD SERIES

Game 3 of the World Series is played on October 20, 1992, at the home of the American League champion Toronto Blue Jays, Skydome in Toronto, Ontario, Canada—the first World Series game played outside the United States. The Blue Jays score a run in the bottom of the ninth to beat the Atlanta Braves 3–2, and go on to win the Series 4–2.

YOU'D THINK THEY'D KNOW BETTER

During the fourth inning of Game 3 of the 1992 World Series in Toronto on October 20, David Justice of the Braves hits a fly ball to deep center field. Deion Sanders is on second and Terry Pendleton is on first with no outs. Sanders retreats to second while Devon White of the Blue Jays fields the ball.

Meanwhile, Pendleton is off with the crack of the bat. Pendleton is called out for passing Sanders.

White makes the catch and relays the ball to Manny Lee for what looks like a triple play. But it is only an extremely unusual World Series double play.

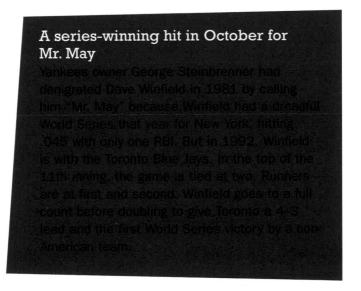

A series-winning hit in October for Mr. May

Yankees owner George Steinbrenner had denigrated Dave Winfield in 1981 by calling him "Mr. May" because Winfield had a dreadful World Series that year for New York, hitting .045 with only one RBI. But in 1992, Winfield is with the Toronto Blue Jays. In the top of the 11th inning, the game is tied at two. Runners are at first and second. Winfield goes to a full count before doubling to give Toronto a 4–3 lead and the first World Series victory by a non-American team.

Gaston's legacy

Clarence "Cito" Gaston is the first black man to manage a team to a pennant as his Toronto Blue Jays win the first of two successive American League pennants and later two World Championships in 1992 and 1993.

A WALK-OFF BLAST

In Game 6, Joe Carter hits a walk-off World Series ending home run off Philadelphia's Mitch Williams to give the Toronto Blue Jays their second consecutive World Championship on October 23, 1993.

EVERY NINETY YEARS

Because of a players' strike, the World Series is cancelled on September 14, 1994—the first year without a World Series since 1904.

YOU'RE GONE. AGAIN

On October 26, 1996, Atlanta Braves manager Bobby Cox sets a dubious record when he becomes the first man ejected from two World Series. The first is on October 20, 1992, in Game 3 against the eventual winner, the Toronto Blue Jays, when he argues a checked-swing call on Jeff Blauser with umpire Joe West in the top of the ninth inning and starts throwing things on the field. Four years later, third-base umpire Tim Welke ejects him for arguing an out call on a steal by Marquis Grissom.

WHAT YOU GET WHEN YOU GOOGLE WADE BOGGS AND HORSE

After the Yankees beat the Braves to win the World Series on October 26, 1996, New York City Police officers, some of them on horses, descend on the field at Yankee Stadium to prevent a repeat of the bedlam which covered the field at Shea Stadium when thousands of fans jumped on to the field to celebrate the Mets victory over the Orioles in the 1969 Series. One of the mounted police officers gives Yankee third baseman Wade Boggs a ride around the field on his horse.

ARE YOU SURE NOBODY'S EVER DONE THIS BEFORE?

Craig Counsell does something on November 4, 2001 which nobody has ever done before: he scores the winning run in the World Series for a second team, the Arizona Diamondbacks, as they beat the Yankees 4 games to 3. In 1997, Counsell had scored the winning run for the Marlins on October 26 as Florida beat the Cleveland Indians 4 games to 3.

How 'bout that!

"Baseball is more than a game. It's a religion."
Bill Klem, Hall of Fame umpire

MERKLE'S BONER

In a Cubs–Giants game at the Polo Grounds on
September 23, 1908, with both teams in the pennant
race, the game is tied at 1 in the bottom of the ninth
inning with two outs and runners on first and third. Al
Bridwell singles to center. Moose McCormick, the
runner on third base, scores with what looks like the
winning run for the Giants. 19-year-old Fred Merkle,
who was on first base, jogs towards second base, but
doesn't touch it. Instead, after he sees McCormick
score what appears to be the winning run, Merkle
turns right to go to the Giants' center field clubhouse.
Cubs second baseman Johnny Evers grabs a ball (it
might even have been the correct ball) and steps on
second base. Umpire Hank O'Day rules that because
Merkle has not touched second base, he is the third
out, the run doesn't count, and the game is still tied.

The Cubs and the Giants finish the season with
identical records of 98–55. The National League
orders the tie game replayed from the time of the
disputed play. The Cubs win the game and the
National League pennant and beat the Detroit Tigers
in the World Series.

Merkle had a fine 16-year career, and although his manager and teammates never blamed him for what came to be called "Merkle's boner," the play followed him to his grave.

Mr. Zero
Ed Reulbach of the Cubs pitches two shutouts on September 26, 1908, beating the Dodgers 5–0 and 3–0. He gives up 8 hits all day.

ON THE BALL
Shortstop Neal Ball of the Cleveland Indians turns an unassisted triple play against the Boston Red Sox on July 19, 1909.

OVER IN A NEW YORK MINUTE
Bill Carrigan of the Red Sox lines into a game-ending triple play (the first triple play ever by the Yankees) on May 6, 1911.

FLASHING SOME LEATHER
Chicago White Sox shortstop Lee Tannehill turns two unassisted double plays in the same game, but the Sox lose 1–0 to Walter Johnson and the Senators, August 4, 1911.

WHO ARE THESE GUYS?

Ty Cobb of the Detroit Tigers is suspended because he climbs into the stands in New York to assault a heckler named Claude Leuker on May 15, 1912. (As it happens, Leuker has no arms. Cobb beats him anyway.) But Cobb's teammates on the Tigers go on strike to support Cobb. On May 18, 1912, in a game against the Athletics in Philadelphia, the Tigers team consists of college players, sandlot players, and Detroit coaches Deacon McGuire and Hughie Jennings. Philadelphia 24, Detroit 2.

The Tigers who play that one game are Ed Irwin, Bill Leinhauser, Billy Maharg, Vincent Maney, Jim McGarr, Dan McGarvey, Jack Smith, Joe Sugden (first game since 1905), Al Travers, and Hap Ward. Their names are all in the record books, and they can tell their grandchildren that they played in the majors. Just not very well.

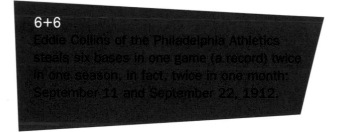

6+6

Eddie Collins of the Philadelphia Athletics steals six bases in one game (a record) twice in one season, in fact, twice in one month: September 11 and September 22, 1912.

TIGER TAMER
CHICK GANDIL OF THE TIGERS LINES TO FRANK BAKER OF THE YANKEES, WHO STARTS A GAME-ENDING TRIPLE PLAY ON JUNE 1, 1918.

Bird on my head
Casey Stengel, an outfielder for the Brooklyn Dodgers, steps out of the Ebbets Field batter's box and removes his hat on June 6, 1918. A bird flies out, cementing Stengel's reputation as a clown.

THAT WAS FAST!
The Giants beat the Phillies 6–1 in 51 minutes on September 28, 1919—the shortest game ever.

CAN'T BUY A HIT
Charlie Pick of the Braves goes a record 0-for-11 on May 1, 1920 in a 26 inning, 1–1 tie game between Boston and Brooklyn. Pitchers Leon Cadore of the Dodgers and Joe Oeschger of the Braves pitch complete games—the longest ever.

A TRAGIC DAY

Pitcher Carl Mays of the Yankees hits Ray Chapman of the Cleveland Indians in the head with a pitch on August 16, 1920. Chapman dies early the next day.

LET'S PLAY THREE

The last tripleheader is played on October 2, 1920. Cincinnati 13, Pittsburgh 4; Cincinnati 7, Pittsburgh 3; Pittsburgh 6, Cincinnati 0. The home plate umpire in all three games is Peter Harrison.

TRADING PLACES

Cliff Heathcote of the Cardinals and Max Flack of the Cubs are traded for each other between games of a doubleheader on May 30, 1922. Both get hits in the second game.

The House That Ruth Built

Yankee Stadium opens on April 18, 1923. The outfield dimensions are fashioned to take advantage of Babe Ruth's left handed swing—hence the name, "The House That Ruth Built." Ruth hits the first home run there as the Yankees beat Boston 4–1.

BY GEORGE
George Burns of the Red Sox turns an unassisted triple play against the Indians on September 14, 1923.

AN UNASSISTED TRIPLE PLAY
Ernie Padgett of the Boston Braves turns an unassisted triple play against the Philadelphia Phillies on October 6, 1923.

> *MOST FAMOUS HEADACHE IN HISTORY*
> *First baseman Wally Pipp of the New York Yankees is kept out of the lineup on June 1, 1925 because of the most famous headache in the history of baseball. The Yankees put Lou Gehrig at first base, where he stays for 2,130 consecutive games.*

IT HAPPENS IN BROOKLYN: BABE HERMAN DOUBLES INTO A DOUBLE PLAY
With the bases loaded at Ebbets Field in Brooklyn on August 15, 1926, Floyd "Babe" Herman of the Dodgers hits a ball to the right field wall. Hank DeBerry scores from third. Dazzy Vance holds up at second base, then tries to score. Chick Fewster, who was on first, stops at third. The throw traps Vance, who retreats to third. Herman slides into third as Fewster steps off the bag. Herman is called out for passing a base runner. Fewster thinks he's out too, so he walks off the field with Herman. He's tagged out. Herman has doubled into a double play.

The Wright way

Glenn Wright of the Pittsburgh Pirates turns an unassisted triple play in the ninth inning on May 7, 1925, against the St. Louis Cardinals. Jimmy Cooney is one of the runners tagged out—see the next entry.

TWO YEARS LATER…

Jimmy Cooney of the Chicago Cubs turns an unassisted triple play against the Pittsburgh Pirates on May 30, 1927. Cooney thus becomes the only man to appear on both sides of an unassisted triple play.

AND THE VERY NEXT DAY…

Johnny Neun of the Detroit Tigers turns an unassisted triple play on May 31, 1927 against the Cleveland Indians.

BANG! OUCH!

Violet Popovich Valli shoots Billy Jurges of the Cubs in his shoulder and hand in a Chicago hotel room on July 6, 1932. He's back with the Cubs in 1933.

HOMETOWN TRIPLE CROWN WINNER

In 1934, Lou Gehrig of the New York Yankees becomes the only man to win the Triple Crown (leading the league with 49 home runs, 165 RBIs, and a batting average of .363) in his hometown, New York City.

RUTH'S LAST BLASTS

Babe Ruth hits three home runs on May 25, 1935, as a Boston Brave. They are career home runs 712, 713, and 714—the last of his career. The final one is the first ball ever hit out of Pittsburgh's Forbes Field.

A PLAYING UMPIRE

John "Jocko" Conlan, a bench warmer for the White Sox, is pressed into service in the second game of a double header after umpire Red Ormsby is overcome by heat prostration on July 28, 1935. Conlan enjoys the experience, umpires in the National League for 25 years, and is inducted into the Hall of Fame as an umpire in 1974.

THREE THE HARD WAY

Joe Cronin of the Red Sox lines into a triple play off the head of Indians pitcher Oral Hildebrand on September 7, 1935.

COMISKEY'S MOST WANTED

Someone in the Comiskey Park stands throws a bottle onto the field on July 26, 1936 during a Yankees–White Sox game. The bottle hits umpire Bill Summers and he's out of the game. Baseball commissioner Kenesaw Mountain Landis, in the stands, uses the public address system to offer a $5,000 reward for the perpetrator. He or she is not identified.

THE IRON MAN FALTERS

Lou Gehrig's streak of 2,130 consecutive games—a mark which seemed unbreakable at the time—ends in Detroit on May 2, 1939, when an ailing Gehrig asks Yankee manager Joe McCarthy to leave his name out of the lineup. He died at the age of 39 on June 2, 1941.

JUNE 6, 1944

All major league games are cancelled today—D–Day.

ONE MORE HIT! ONE MORE HIT!

Frank Demaree of the St. Louis Browns, an All-Star in 1936 and 1937 plays the final game of his 12-year career on June 13, 1944. He goes 0-for-3, leaving his batting average at .29947, rounded off to .299. One hit more than the 1,241 he accumulated would have made him a career .300 hitter.

THREE TEAMS, NOT A TRIPLEHEADER

It's not a tripleheader, but three New York teams played six innings each at the Polo Grounds in New York on June 26, 1944 in a war bonds fund raiser. Final score: Dodgers 5, Yankees 1, Giants 0.

Meet Pete Gray

Because many major league players are still in the service, ballclubs are desperate for players. On April 17, 1945, 30-year-old Pete Gray (Wyshner) makes his major league debut for the St. Louis Browns. Gray has only one arm—the left one. When the regulars return for the 1946 season, Gray's big league career—.218, six doubles, three triples, and five stolen bases—is over too.

AN UNUSUAL BIRTHPLACE

Future Hall of Famer Rod Carew is born on a moving train near Gatun, Panama on October 1, 1945.

NO HOME FIELD ADVANTAGE

While the newly-painted seats dry at Braves Field on April 28, 1946, the Boston Braves "host" the Philadelphia Phillies across town at Fenway Park.

NO DAY GAMES TODAY
For the first time in history, on August 9, 1946
all major league games are night games.

BABE RUTH'S SPEECH

"Babe Ruth Day" is held at at Yankee Stadium on April 27, 1947. During his farewell speech, Ruth says: "The only real game, I think, in the world, is baseball."

NEVER GIVE UP

Lou Brissie makes his major league debut on September 28, 1947 with the Philadelphia As. Brissie is severely wounded by artillery fire in Italy during World War II. His left ankle and right foot are broken, and his left shinbone is shattered into more than 30 pieces. He is one of the first patients to receive the new miracle drug penicillin. Brissie perseveres, and pitches 234 games for the Philadelphia Athletics and Cleveland Indians.

Indian summer

The race for the American League pennant comes down to a one-game playoff on October 4, 1948. The Cleveland Indians beat the Red Sox 8–3 for the pennant.

What, another flagpole-sitter?

For 117 days starting in May, 1949, Charley Lupica, an Indians fan, sits atop a flagpole in a little treehouse, vowing not to come down until the Indians are in first place. Thanks to team owner Bill Veeck, he and the "house" are removed and taken to Cleveland's Municipal Stadium for the last game of the season, so the fans could see him. The Indians finished in third place, eight games behind the Yankees.

NO ZOOM, JUST BANG!

Ann Steinhagen shoots Phillies first baseman "Big" Eddie Waitkus on June 15, 1949 in her Chicago hotel room. She is found insane and committed to an institution. Waitkus returns to baseball in 1950 and plays six more seasons.

I'M BAAAAAACK!

After missing the first 65 games of the season with a painful sore heel, Joe DiMaggio wakes up on June 28, 1949, pain-free. He returns to the lineup that night with a bang—a homer and a single, and smacks four homers in a three-game sweep of the Red Sox in Boston.

AMBIDEXTROUS FIRST PITCHES
AT THE WASHINGTON SENATORS OPENING DAY ON APRIL 18, 1950, PRESIDENT HARRY S. TRUMAN THROWS OUT TWO CEREMONIAL FIRST PITCHES— ONE LEFTY AND ONE RIGHTY.

A short major league career
3'7" tall Eddie Gaedel bats for the St. Louis Browns on August 19, 1951. He walks on four pitches from Bob Cain of the Detroit Tigers. Gaedel wears uniform #⅛—the only fractional uniform number in history. Gaedel's uniform shirt is on display at the Baseball Hall of Fame.

LET'S ALL MANAGE THE TEAM
It's tough to decide which of Bill Veeck's stunts is the wackiest. How about the one he pulls on August 24, 1951, when he asks 1,115 St. Louis Browns fans to hold up signs saying either YES or NO when the coaches question them about such tactics as bunts, intentional walks, and the like. Veeck has the team's manager, Zack Taylor sit in the stands and count the votes. It must have worked: Browns 5, Philadelphia As 3.

One stadium, one day, two games, three teams
The scene: Sportsman's Park, St. Louis. The date: September 13, 1951. A rainout the previous day causes a Cardinals–Giants game to be played before the regularly scheduled Cardinals–Braves game. Final score: Giants 6, Cardinals 4; Braves 2, Cardinals 0.

THAT MAN!

Stan "The Man" Musial of the St. Louis Cardinals puts on an awesome display of power, hitting five home runs (3 in the first, and 2 in the second) in a double header against the Giants on May 2, 1954.

OUCH!

On May 7, 1957, Gil McDougald of the Yankees hits a comebacker which strikes Indians pitcher Herb Score in the right eye. Score's nose is broken, too. Score is out for the season, but returns in 1958.

OUCH! OUCH!

Richie Ashburn of the Phillies achieves a dubious distinction when he hits the same fan with foul balls twice in one at-bat. On August 17, 1957, at Philadelphia's Shibe Park, the first one breaks Alice Roth's nose. As she is being removed from the stands on a stretcher, Ashburn hits her with a second foul ball.

A TRAGIC ACCIDENT

While driving home on an icy road on January 28, 1958, Dodgers catcher Roy Campanella's car skids and hits a telephone pole. He fractures his fifth cervical vertebra, injures his spinal cord, and is permanently paralyzed from the neck down. Campanella was the first black catcher in the major leagues, a three-time Most Valuable Player and a Hall of Famer. More than that, he is a universally loved and respected player.

THAT'S USING YOUR HEAD

BATTING HELMETS BECOME MANDATORY IN THE AMERICAN LEAGUE ON MARCH 11, 1958.

NOW THAT'S A CROWD!

93,103 fans—the largest crowd in baseball history—gather at the Los Angeles Coliseum, the temporary home of the Dodgers, on May 7, 1959: "Roy Campanella Night." The Yankees beat the Dodgers 6–2 in an exhibition game.

TRADED FOR HIMSELF

On April 26, 1962, the Indians trade Harry Chiti to the New York Mets for a player to be named later. On June 15, the Mets designate the player to be named later: Harry Chiti.

WHAT A WAY TO GO!

In the last at-bat of his career, Joe Pignatano of the New York Mets hits into a triple play by the Chicago Cubs on September 30, 1962.

Run, Maury, run

The Most Valuable Player in the National League in 1962 hit only .299 with no home runs. He is not a pitcher. But Maury Wills brings back the lost art of base-stealing by stealing 104 bases and scoring 130 runs for the Los Angeles Dodgers as they finished second in the National League.

BROTHERS IN THE OUTFIELD

For the only time in history, in the seventh inning of a Giants–Mets game on September 22, 1963, the three outfield positions are manned by three brothers—Matty Alou in left, Felipe Alou in center (replacing Willie Mays), and Jesus Alou in right. The three brothers go down in order in the eighth inning, but their Giants win 13–4.

THE MOST INFAMOUS MUSICIAN IN BASEBALL HISTORY

The Yankees pile on to the team bus after a 5–0 loss to the White Sox on August 20, 1964. Phil Linz starts playing "Mary Had a Little Lamb" on his harmonica. Manager Yogi Berra, still upset over the loss, shouts from his front row seat that Linz should stop playing. But Linz doesn't hear Berra, and asks Mickey Mantle, in the seat next to him, "What did Yogi say?" Mantle tells Linz: "He wants you to play louder!" When Linz does play louder, Berra storms back to Linz's seat, grabs the harmonica, and throws it down on the floor of the bus. Shortly after the incident is reported, Linz is offered a contract by a harmonica manufacturer.

THE WILD WEST

Juan Marichal of the Giants is batting in San Francisco when Dodgers catcher John Roseboro throws a ball back to the pitcher on August 22, 1965. Marichal thinks the throw is too close to his head, so he hits Roseboro over the head with his bat. Twice. The benches empty for a 14-minute fight as Roseboro bleeds from a two-inch gash in his head. Marichal is later suspended for eight games and fined.

MR. VERSATILITY

BERT CAMPANERIS OF THE As PLAYS ALL NINE POSITIONS IN ONE GAME ON SEPTEMBER 8, 1965— THE FIRST MAN TO DO SO.

What did not happen in the opening game of the 1965 World Series

What didn't happen is that the star pitcher for the Los Angeles Dodgers, Sandy Koufax, did not pitch. The game is played on October 6, 1965—Yom Kippur, the Jewish Day of Atonement. Koufax, who is Jewish, sits it out, and Don Drysdale pitches instead. The Twins win 8–2, but the Dodgers take the Series 4–3. Koufax loses Game 2, but wins games 5 and 7. It's nice when your #1 and #2 starters are both bound for the Hall of Fame.

BEANED

Tony Conigliaro, slugging star of the pennant-bound Boston Red Sox, is hit just below his left eye by a pitch from Jack Hamilton of the Angels on August 18, 1967. Tony C misses the rest of the season, and all of 1968.

HEY, YOU CAN'T EJECT ME—THE GAME HASN'T EVEN STARTED YET!

John Boozer of the Phillies is ejected for throwing spitball warm-up pitches before the second game of a doubleheader on May 1, 1968.

Have a cigar

Jeff Bagwell, National League Most Valuable Player in 1994 as the first baseman for the Houston Astros, and Frank Thomas, American League Most Valuable Player in 1994 as the first baseman for the Chicago White Sox are born nine hours and 28 minutes apart on May 27, 1968. Thomas: 4:35 A.M., Bagwell: 2:03 P.M.

> *CAPITAL PUNISHMENT*
> *Ron Hansen of the Washington Senators turns the first unassisted triple play in 41 years against the Cleveland Indians on July 30, 1968.*

BREAKS OF THE GAME

Phillies catcher Tim McCarver breaks his hand when he's hit by a foul tip in the sixth inning on May 2, 1970 at San Francisco. Mike Ryan replaces McCarver behind the plate. Later in the same inning, Willie McCovey of the Giants is thrown out at the plate while trying to score. In the process, McCovey spikes Ryan, breaking his hand. One inning, two catchers, two broken hands.

HEAD OVER HEELS

Trying to score in the bottom of the 12th inning of the All-Star Game on July 14, 1970, in Cincinnati, Pete Rose of the National League Cincinnati Reds runs at full speed and bowls over catcher Ray Fosse of the American League Cleveland Indians. Rose's run is the game-winner, as the National League wins 5–4. Fosse is never the same after the play.

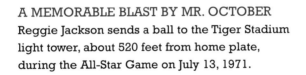

A MEMORABLE BLAST BY MR. OCTOBER

Reggie Jackson sends a ball to the Tiger Stadium light tower, about 520 feet from home plate, during the All-Star Game on July 13, 1971.

WILLIE'S BACK

After his dramatic May 11, 1972 trade from the San Francisco Giants to the New York Mets, Willie Mays makes his triumphant first appearance in a major league uniform which does not say GIANTS on it. On May 14, 1972, Mays homers for the Mets to help beat the Giants 5–4.

WHY BOTHER WITH COLLEGE OR THE MINORS?

Just 20 days after pitching for his high school team, David Clyde, who was given a signing bonus of $125,000, makes his major league debut for the Texas Rangers on June 27, 1973. Clyde wins the game and goes on to a 18–33 record in five years.

AN UNUSUAL BIRTHPLACE

Future major league pitcher Danny Graves is born on August 7, 1973 in Saigon, South Vietnam.

AN INFAMOUS BRAWL

The Mets are ahead of the Reds 9–2 in the fifth inning of Game 3 of the National League Championship Series at New York's Shea Stadium on October 8, 1973. Pete Rose is the runner on first base when a ball is hit to Mets first baseman John Milner, who throws to shortstop Bud Harrelson. Harrelson steps on second for the out. As he throws to first to complete a double play, Rose slides into him. Hard. Harrelson goes down. The two fight ferociously but without serious injury. The only real injury is to a Mets hat, which Pedro Borbon rips apart with his teeth. The game resumes, but when Rose takes his position in left field in the bottom of the inning, he is showered with debris—including a whiskey bottle—from the stands. The Reds leave the field. They return with police surrounding the playing field. Final score: Mets 9, Reds 2. The Mets win the National League Championship Series 3–2.

GOOD RUN, NO HIT

Herb Washington makes his debut with the Oakland Athletics on April 4, 1974—the only "designated runner" in the history of the game. Washington, a world-class sprinter with virtually no baseball experience, scores 33 runs in two years with 31 stolen bases, no hits, and no at-bats.

You've had enough

60,000 beers are sold at Cleveland's Municipal Stadium on "10¢ Beer Night," June 4, 1974. Over 25,000 fans attend, but they are so unruly that with the game tied at five in the bottom of the ninth inning the umpires declare a forfeit to the Rangers.

FEELING LIKE A MILLION

On May 4, 1975, Bob Watson of the Houston Astros scores what is said to be the millionth run in baseball since 1876, when "official" records started.

LET'S HEAR IT FOR TEENS

COOPERSTOWN-BOUND ROBIN YOUNT OF THE MILWAUKEE BREWERS SETS THE RECORD FOR MOST MAJOR LEAGUE GAMES PLAYED BY A TEENAGER— 242—ON SEPTEMBER 14, 1975.

You're a grand old flag

In the fourth inning of a Cubs–Dodgers game in Los Angeles on April 25, 1976, two vandals jump onto the field at Dodger Stadium from the left field corner and head for left centerfield. There, they unfurl an American flag and pour lighter fluid on it. One of them strikes a match and tries to set the flag on fire. But the match flickers out. As he reaches for another, Rick Monday, the Cubs center fielder and a six-year member of the United States Marine Corps Reserves, runs towards them at full speed and knocks the vandal over, preventing him from igniting the flag. Monday grabs it and gives the flag to Dodger pitcher Doug Rau. The flag is later presented to Monday. The Illinois Legislature declares May 4, 1976, as Rick Monday Day.

NO LOVE LOST

Lou Piniella of the Yankees, trying to score, knocks over Red Sox catcher Carlton Fisk at Yankee Stadium. They go at each other as both benches clear. Boston pitcher Bill "Spaceman" Lee is body-slammed during the melee and breaks his collarbone. And it's not even the postseason: the game is played on May 20, 1976.

OH, BROTHER!

Pitcher Joe Niekro of the Houston Astros, a veteran of 9 years in the major leagues, hits the only home run of his career on May 29, 1976. The pitcher? His brother Phil of the Atlanta Braves.

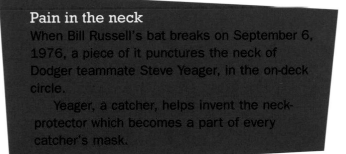

Pain in the neck

When Bill Russell's bat breaks on September 6, 1976, a piece of it punctures the neck of Dodger teammate Steve Yeager, in the on-deck circle.

Yeager, a catcher, helps invent the neck-protector which becomes a part of every catcher's mask.

APPARENTLY ANY IDIOT CAN MANAGE

Ted Turner, owner of the Atlanta Braves, became Ted Turner, manager of the Atlanta Braves for one game, in uniform, on May 11, 1977 as the Braves suffer their 17th straight loss, 2–1, to the Pirates in Pittsburgh. He is fined because owners are prohibited from the dugout and from managing.

A Royal pain

John Wathan of the Royals hits into an unusual game-ending triple play turned by the Baltimore Orioles on June 3, 1977. Wathan, pinch-hitting, hits a sacrifice fly to right field, scoring Al Cowens, but Dave Nelson and Fred Patek are retired on the basepaths as the Royals lose 7–6.

HEY YOU KIDS! MAKE SURE THIS DOES NOT HAPPEN TO YOU

At Fenway Park in Boston, Reggie Jackson is playing right field for the New York Yankees on June 18, 1977. He misplays a popup by Jim Rice of the Red Sox. Manager Billy Martin sends Paul Blair out to right and pulls Jackson off the field. When Jackson returns to the dugout, the two almost come to blows, and have to be restrained by coaches Yogi Berra and Elston Howard. The entire confrontation is broadcast on network television.

STEALING HIS WAY INTO YOUR HEART AND INTO THE HALL OF FAME

Lou Brock of the Cardinals records career stolen base #893 on August 29, 1977, breaking Ty Cobb's modern record.

C'MON, LET'S GO
Baltimore manager Earl Weaver pulls his team off the field in Toronto on September 15, 1977, and the Orioles forfeit. Weaver's complaints about the danger created by bricks holding down a bullpen tarp were ignored.

Thanks, Brooks
51,798 fans, the largest crowd in the history of Baltimore's Memorial Stadium gather on September 18, 1977 for "Thanks, Brooks" Night to pay homage to future Hall of Famer Brooks Robinson, who is retiring after 23 years, all with the Orioles.

QUITE A SHOW
During a rain delay at Fenway Park on October 1, 1977, Rick Dempsey of the Baltimore Orioles stuffs a pillow in his shirt and rounds the bases (which are covered by a tarp) belly-flopping into each one.

GAME OVER
Ron Cey of the Los Angeles Dodgers hits into a game-ending triple play turned by the Houston Astros on April 21, 1978.

MENTION MY NAME IN SHEBOYGAN,
BUT NOT IN NEW ENGLAND

Very few players have a name that is anathema in an entire part of the country. But on October 2, 1978 Bucky Dent achieves that status in New England and gains an unprintable middle name there with his seventh inning, three-run home run off Mike Torrez of the Red Sox in Boston in the one-game playoff to decide the American League East championship. The Yankees go on to defeat the Red Sox 5–4. Because of the historic rivalry between the teams, the drama created because it's a one-game playoff, the Yankees' comeback from 14 games behind the Red Sox, and the palpable excitement of every pitch, every swing, every hit, this game is one of the most memorable in baseball's long history.

BOOM!

As a promotion to draw fans to Chicago's Comiskey Park, a local disc jockey and Mike Veeck, son of Bill Veeck, the team owner, stage Disco Demolition Night. The promoters tell fans that any disco records they brought would be blown up between games of a White Sox–Tigers doubleheader. Nearly 48,000 fans show up on July 12, 1979. Admission is 98¢ with a disco record. The explosion and fans on the field leave so much debris that the field is declared unplayable. The second game is cancelled and the Tigers are awarded a victory by forfeit.

ST. LOU
LOU BROCK OF THE CARDINALS SMASHES
HIS 3,000TH HIT ON AUGUST 13, 1979, ON
HIS WAY TO 3,023.

BROCK'S LAST STEAL
Lou Brock of the St. Louis Cardinals steals the last
base of his career on September 23, 1979—#938.

We want Minnie! We want Minnie!
Saturnino Orestes Armas Minoso Arrieta, better
known as Minnie Minoso of the Chicago White Sox
comes to bat for the 6,579th and final time on
October 5, 1980. His at-bat means that the soon to
be 57-year-old Minoso has played in five decades:
1940s, 1950s, 1960s, 1970s, and 1980s.

ROYALTY
The Kansas City Royals lose the American League
Championship Series to the New York Yankees in
1976, 1977, and 1978. In Game 3 of the 1980 Series
on October 10, George Brett comes to bat in the top
of the seventh inning to face Rich "Goose" Gossage
of the Yankees. The Royals are behind 2–1, but Brett's
titanic homer to right field leads to a 4–2 K.C. win.
The Royals sweep the Yankees 3–0 in the best of five
series, but lose the World Series 4–2 to the Phillies.

SO LONG...

The longest game in the history of professional baseball starts on April 18, 1981 in Pawtucket, Rhode Island. The International League game between the Pawtucket Red Sox and the Rochester Red Wings is tied at 2 in the 32nd inning at 4:07 A.M. when play is suspended. When it is completed later in the season, Pawtucket scores a run to win in the 33rd inning. Cal Ripken, Jr. (Red Wings) and Wade Boggs (Red Sox) play in the game.

GOING, GOING, GONE!

During an Old Timers' Game at Washington, D.C.'s RFK Stadium on July 19, 1982, 77-year-old Hall of Famer Luke Appling homers off another Hall of Famer, Warren Spahn.

HE CAN REST IN NOVEMBER

Starting on Opening Day, April 4, 1983, and through the final game of the World Series, October 16, Cal Ripken, Jr. of the Baltimore Orioles becomes the first man to play in every inning of every game for his team— all 171 games. (162 in the regular season, 4 in the playoffs, and 5 in the Series.) The Orioles beat the Philadelphia Phillies 4–1.

Ouch!

On August 4, 1983, Dave Winfield of the Yankees finishes his warmup throws in left field at Exhibition Stadium in Toronto. He throws a ball which hits and kills a seagull (a protected species in Ontario) and is arrested for causing "unnecessary suffering to an animal" and handcuffed. The charges are later dismissed because the incident was deemed an accident.

STEVIE WONDER

The Cubs led the 1984 National League Championship Series 2–1 over San Diego. In the bottom of the ninth inning of the fourth game, Steve Garvey homers to give the Padres a 7–5 win and even the series. San Diego wins the decisive Game 5, but loses the World Series 4–1 to the Detroit Tigers.

WHAT A DAY FOR PITCHING AND HITTING!

In New York, Tom Seaver of the White Sox beats the Yankees to win his 300th game on August 4, 1985. On the same day in Anaheim, Rod Carew of the Angels gets his 3,000th hit.

Look out for that tarp!

Vince Coleman of the Cardinals is stretching before Game 4 of the National League Championship Series at Busch Stadium in St. Louis, October 3, 1985. His leg is caught in the automatic tarpaulin as it moves across the field, and Coleman is trapped underneath it for 30 seconds. The injury ends his season, and he misses the World Series, which the Cardinals lose 4–3 to the Kansas City Royals.

EIGHT IS ENOUGH

Don Mattingly of the New York Yankees connects for a home run in his eighth consecutive game on July 18, 1987, tying a record set by Dale Long of the Pittsburgh Pirates in 1956.

Hot potato

Dave Bresnahan, catcher for the Williamsport Bills of the Class "AA" Eastern League, hides a peeled potato in his mitt on August 31, 1987. With a runner on third, he throws the potato wildly to third base. When the runner sees the wide throw, he breaks for home, only to be tagged out by a perfect throw from the pitcher home—with an actual baseball. The umpires eventually call the runner safe, the run scores, and Bresnahan is both fined and fired. His pro baseball career is over.

Last place MVP

For the first time in history, a player on a last place team is voted the league's Most Valuable Player on November 18, 1987 leaving unanswered the question, "Couldn't they have finished last without him?"

Andre Dawson (.287, 49 home runs, 137 RBIs) of the Chicago Cubs (76–85, 18 games behind the division-leading Cardinals) is voted the Most Valuable Player in the National League.

40-40

José Canseco of the Oakland As becomes the first player with 40 homers and 40 stolen bases in a single season on September 24, 1988, as he steals bases #39 and #40.

MARRIED AT THE OLD OFFICE

FORMER PITCHING STAR VIDA BLUE AND PEGGY SHANNON ARE MARRIED ON SEPTEMBER 24, 1989 ON THE PITCHER'S MOUND AT CANDLESTICK PARK IN SAN FRANCISCO BEFORE A CROWD OF 50,000.

DON'T HIT IT TO HIM

Third baseman Gary Gaetti of the Minnesota Twins starts two triple plays in a game against the Boston Red Sox, but the Sox still win on July 17, 1990.

WHY DO YOU THINK THEY CALL HIM "PSYCHO"?

While smoothing out his uniform after reaching first base on August 13, 1990, Steve Lyons of the Chicago White Sox drops his pants. On television.

EVERY FATHER'S DREAM
Ken Griffey, Sr. has an experience which has been the dream of virtually every father who has ever played in the major leagues: In his first game with the Seattle Mariners, on August 31, 1990, one of his teammates is his son, Ken, Jr.

IT TAKES A THIEF
IT'S CAREER STOLEN BASE #1,000 FOR THE OAKLAND AS' RICKEY HENDERSON ON MAY 1, 1992.

SLIPPING THEM A MICKEY
Mickey Morandini, second baseman for the Philadelphia Phillies, turns the first unassisted triple play in 24 years against the Pittsburgh Pirates on September 23, 1992.

IT'S BASEBALL, NOT SOCCER
In the fourth inning of an Indians–Rangers game, Texas outfielder José Canseco misplays a drive by Carlos Martinez on May 26, 1993. The ball bounces off Canseco's head and over the fence for a home run. The Rangers lose 7–6.

CATCHING ON

Carlton Fisk of the Chicago White Sox catches his 2,226th game, breaking the previous record held by Bob Boone on June 22, 1993. It is Fisk's last game.

Homer. Homer. Homer.

Opening Day: April 4, 1994. Karl "Tuffy" Rhodes of the Chicago Cubs hits home runs in his first three at-bats of the season—the first player to do so. But the Cubs lose 12–8 to the Mets.

OOSP!

JOE CARTER OF THE BLUE JAYS PLAYS IN A UNIFORM SHIRT WHICH SAYS "TOROTNO" ON JULY 14, 1994.

VALENTIN'S DAY

John Valentin of the Boston Red Sox turns an unassisted triple play against the Minnesota Twins on July 15, 1994.

NOT HAVING A BALL

Raul Mondesi of the Los Angeles Dodgers argues a strike three call and is ejected on August 10, 1995: "Ball Day" at Dodger Stadium. L.A. manager Tommy Lasorda joins the argument and is also thrown out of the game. The fans are displeased with the ejections and shower the field with approximately 200 free souvenir balls. The Cardinals are ordered into their dugout and they win by forfeit.

AN "UNBREAKABLE" RECORD IS BROKEN

Cal Ripken, Jr. of the Baltimore Orioles plays in his 2,131st consecutive game on September 6, 1995, breaking the previously thought-to-be-unbreakable record set by Lou Gehrig of the New York Yankees from 1925 to 1939.

PTUEY!

Roberto Alomar of the Baltimore Orioles spits in the face of umpire John Hirschbeck on September 27, 1996. Alomar is eventually suspended for five games.

Home field advantage

In Game 1 of the 1996 American League Championship Series on October 9, Derek Jeter of the Yankees hits a deep fly ball to right field at Yankee Stadium. As Orioles right fielder Tony Tarasco tries to catch it, somebody else makes the catch—Jeffrey Maier, a 12-year-old fan in the stands who reaches over the wall to make the play. Despite Tarasco's protests, it's called (probably erroneously) a home run by umpire Rich Garcia. Yankees win the game 5–4 and the series 4–1.

SWITCH!

After 27 years in the American League, the Milwaukee Brewers switch to the National League in 1997.

Harry and son

In a Padres–Marlins game in San Diego on August 10, 1998, umpire Harry Wendelstedt is behind the plate and his son Hunter umpires at second base—the first time a father and son umpire in the same major league game.

THE ALL-BROTHER INFIELD

The Reds infield on September 27, 1998 contains a first: two sets of brothers. Stephen Larkin plays first base, while his brother Barry is at short. Aaron Boone is at third, and his brother Bret is at second.

THE STREAK ENDS

After 2,632 consecutive games for the Baltimore Orioles, Cal Ripken, Jr. decides on September 20, 1998 to end his streak and he stays on the bench. The streak began on May 30, 1982.

FAREWELL, MICK

Hall of Famer Mickey Mantle dies in Dallas, Texas on August 13, 1995 at the age of 64 after a second liver transplant fails.

> *SCRUB THE D.H.*
>
> *When designated hitter José Canseco goes in to play left field for the Red Sox on May 23, 1996, they lose the D.H. The pitcher, Roger Clemens, comes to bat for the first time in his career. Clemens singles and earns a complete game 11–4 win over the Seattle Mariners.*

WHO SAYS BASEBALL IS NOT EXCITING?

The Red Sox–White Sox game on June 6, 1996, won by the Red Sox 7–4, features two rare occurrences: a triple play turned by the White Sox, and Boston's John Valentin hitting for the cycle.

THERE'S A TIME FOR ARGUING AND A TIME FOR PLAYING

In the top of the 12th inning in Game 2 of the American League championship Series, on October 7, 1998, Travis Fryman of the Indians bunts up the first base line. Yankee first baseman Tino Martinez fields the ball, and throws to second baseman Chuck Knoblauch, covering first. But the ball hits Fryman and rolls towards right field. Instead of fielding the ball, Knoblauch argues with first base umpire John

Shulock that interference should have been called on Fryman, who is still running. The ball just sits there. Enrique Wilson, who had been on first, does not argue the call. He circles the bases and scores. It's a three-run inning for Cleveland. The Yankees lose the game, 4–1, but win the ALCS 4–2, prior to sweeping the Padres 4–0 in the World Series.

WHO'S THAT MAN IN THE SUNGLASSES?

Mets manager Bobby Valentine is ejected in the 12th inning of a game on June 9, 1999, by umpire Randy Marsh for arguing a catcher's interference call on Mike Piazza. Valentine returns to the Mets dugout later in what he thought was a disguise— sunglasses, a non-Mets hat, and an eye-black mustache. Valentine is fined $5,000 and suspended for two games for this disgraceful but memorable stunt.

A BAD DAY FOR CHILI

CHARLES "CHILI" DAVIS OF THE YANKEES HITS INTO A TRIPLE PLAY AND A DOUBLE PLAY ON JUNE 17, 1999.

MOST MEMORABLE MOMENT IN THE MOST MEMORABLE ALL-STAR GAME

The place: Fenway Park. The occasion: the All-Star Game. The date: July 13, 1999. The moment: On the field where he played for 19 years, surrounded by such baseball immortals as Hank Aaron, Bob Feller, Carlton Fisk, Willie Mays, Reggie Jackson, Barry Bonds, Pete Rose, Stan Musial, Tony Gwynn, Cal Ripken, Jr., Bob Gibson, Randy Johnson, Roger Clemens, Mike Piazza, Curt Schilling, Sammy Sosa, Ken Griffey, Jr., Rafael Palmeiro, Ivan Rodriguez, Mark McGwire, Pedro Martinez, Orlando Cepeda, Nomar Garciaparra, and Derek Jeter, an ailing 80-year-old Ted Williams is driven onto the field in a golf cart from center field to the pitcher's mound to throw out the ceremonial first pitch.

You do a good Nomar Garciaparra

Derek Jeter bats during the fourth inning of the July 13, 1999 All-Star Game, having succeeded Boston's Nomar Garciaparra at shortstop. Before stepping into the batter's box, Jeter does a perfect imitation of Garciaparra's pre-batting rituals: restrapping his gloves, checking his helmet, bat, shoes, socks, adjusting every article of clothing, then rocking back and forth 437 times from his toes to his heels. Then Jeter strikes out.

AN UNUSUAL ROOKIE DEBUT

35-year-old Jim Morris makes his debut pitching for the Tampa Bay Devil Rays, September 18, 1999. Morris goes to a tryout camp on a dare from the students in his high school science class. Morris appears in 21 games until arm trouble ends his career. Dennis Quaid plays Morris in the aptly named film, *The Rookie*.

Heads up!

Yankee bench coach Don Zimmer is seated— on the bench, of course—in the dugout at Yankee Stadium when a foul ball off the bat of Chuck Knoblauch hits him in the face during Game 1 of the American League Division Series against the Texas Rangers on October 5, 1999. The ball cuts his jaw and his ear, and he is bleeding as he is helped from the dugout. The next day, Zimmer, 68, sits in the dugout wearing an army helmet with the Yankee logo. The following year, the Stadium dugouts are protected by fences.

DANDY RANDY

ON MAY 29, 2000, RANDY VELARDE OF THE OAKLAND ATHLETICS TURNS AN UNASSISTED TRIPLE PLAY AGAINST THE NEW YORK YANKEES.

COLOR ME EMBARRASSED!

Name a way not to celebrate July 4, 2000. Ken Griffey, Jr. of the Reds loses his grip on his bat while swinging for a pitch. The bat flies out of his hands—right into the forehead of 10-year-old Christine Lindner, seated in the front row by the Reds dugout. She needs eight stitches. Christine's grandfather Carl is the CEO of the Reds.

An unusual doubleheader

The Yankees and the Mets play a doubleheader on July 8, 2000. The Yankees win the first game 4–2 at Shea Stadium and the second game by the same score at Yankee Stadium. In the second game, Roger Clemens hits Mike Piazza in the head with a pitch, giving him a concussion.

THAT'S GOTTA HURT

Red Sox pitcher Bryce Florie is hit in the face by a comebacker off the bat of by Ryan Thompson of the Yankees at Fenway Park on September 8, 2000. The smash breaks Florie's cheekbone and eye socket, and injures his retina. He undergoes surgery, but is back on the mound in 2001.

SPLIT DECISION

The Cleveland Indians play two different teams at Jacobs Field on September 25, 2000. First, they beat the White Sox 9–2. Then they lose to the Twins, 4–3.

WALK LIKE A MAN
RICKEY HENDERSON OF THE SAN DIEGO PADRES WALKS FOR THE 2,063TH TIME IN HIS CAREER ON APRIL 25, 2001, BREAKING BABE RUTH'S RECORD, WHICH HAD STOOD FOR 66 YEARS.

LOOK OUT, TOMMY!
Honorary National League coach Tommy Lasorda of the Dodgers coaches third base during the 2001 All-Star Game on July 11 at Safeco Field in Seattle. In the sixth inning, Vladimir Guerrero bats against Mike Stanton, and breaks his bat. The bat hits Lasorda in the stomach and knocks him down head over heels. But the 73-year-old Lasorda is unhurt and stays in the game.

RIJO'S RETURN
Jose Rijo, hobbled by health problems, returns to the majors for the first time in six years and pitches for the Reds on August 17, 2001.

OLDEST PLAYER IN THE 20-20 CLUB
Paul O'Neill, 38, of the New York Yankees becomes the oldest man to join the 20-20 club when he hits his 20th home run of the season on August 25, 2001, to go with his 20 stolen bases.

RUN, RICKEY!

41-year-old Rickey Henderson scores the 2,246th run of his career, breaking Ty Cobb's record on October 4, 2001. He extends that mark to 2,295 through the end of the 2003 season, Henderson's last.

Welcome to November baseball

After the attacks of September 11, 2001, all baseball games are cancelled through September 16. The World Series does not start until October 27.

Game 4 of the Series between the Arizona Diamondbacks and the New York Yankees starts on the evening of October 31, 2001 (Halloween) at Yankee Stadium.

Derek Jeter comes to bat in the bottom of the tenth inning with the game tied at three, two out, and nobody on base. The Yankee Stadium clock shows the time: 12 midnight. The scoreboard reads, "ATTENTION FANS: WELCOME TO NOVEMBER BASEBALL!" Jeter homers off Byung-Hyun Kim to end the game—the first home run ever hit in November.

WHAT A PLAY!

In Game 3 of the American League Division Series between the New York Yankees and the Athletics in Oakland, on October 13, 2001, the Yankees are ahead 1–0 in the seventh inning with two outs. Jeremy Giambi is the runner on first base. Terrence Long hits a liner to right which is fielded by Shane Spencer of the Yankees. He overthrows two cutoff men, but shortstop Derek Jeter, playing miles out of position, grabs the ball between home plate and first and backhands it to Jorge Posada who blindly tags out Giambi trying to score. It is one of the great plays of all time.

500 + 500

Barry Bonds steals his 500th base on June 23, 2003 at San Francisco, becoming the first man to hit 500 home runs and steal 500 bases.

TURNING THREE

On August 10, 2003, Rafael Furcal of the Atlanta Braves turns an unassisted triple play against the St. Louis Cardinals.

Don Zimmer can't take out Pedro Martinez either

During the fourth inning of Game 3 of the American League Championship Series between the New York Yankees and the Boston Red Sox at Fenway Park on October 12, 2003, 72-year-old Yankees bench coach Don Zimmer runs at and tries to attack Red Sox pitcher Pedro Martinez. Zimmer thinks that Martinez has been throwing at Yankee batters. As he nears the pitcher, Martinez pushes Zimmer to the ground and Zimmer is helped from the field. The next day, an embarrassed Zimmer apologizes.

FIVE OUTS AWAY

It's Game 6 of the National League Championship Series, Marlins vs. Cubs, October 14, 2003. The Cubs lead the series 3–2, and are ahead 3–0 in the top of the eighth inning. The Cubs are five outs away from winning the series and advancing to the World Series. The Wrigley Field fans are chanting "FIVE MORE OUTS! FIVE MORE OUTS!" With a runner on second, Florida's Luis Castillo hits a high foul ball towards the left field seats—a ball which is apparently catchable. Cubs left fielder Moises Alou moves towards the stands, and makes a play for the ball. But Steve Bartman, a Cubs fan sitting in the front row, reaches out and tries to catch the ball. He doesn't catch it, but he does deflect it. No catch. No out. The Marlins go on to score eight runs in the inning, winning the game 8–3, win Game 7 the following night, the NLCS, and the World Series too.

In a stirring ceremony, the "Bartman Ball" is later detonated. Its remnants are on display in the three Harry Caray restaurants in and around Chicago.

As for Bartman himself, he receives death threats and has the honor of being denounced by the governor of Illinois. The governor of Florida offered him asylum. He has apologized for his actions, but probably won't return to Wrigley Field until the Cubs are in the World Series.

BOONE SOCKS THE SOX

The Boston Red Sox face their long-time nemesis, the New York Yankees in the American League Championship Series of 2003—the winner to go to the World Series. The ALCS goes to the bottom of the 11th inning in Game 7 on October 16, when Aaron Boone (who hit .176 for the series) hits a walk-off home run before 56,000 screaming fans.

THE BEST ON THE WORST

Alex Rodriguez wins the American League Most Valuable Player Award for 2003. His statistics are excellent: .298 batting average, 47 home runs, and 118 RBIs. But they are not enough to help his team, the Texas Rangers, who finish last in the American League West, 71–91, 25 games behind the Oakland As.

HOW CAN YOU BE SO STUPID?

New York Yankees pitcher Kevin Brown, who is paid $15,000,000 per year to pitch, is upset with himself for a subpar performance on September 3, 2004. So he bangs his left (non-pitching) hand against the clubhouse wall, breaking two bones. While his team is in a pennant race, Brown undergoes surgery.

TWO NATIONAL LEAGUE TEAMS IN AN AMERICAN LEAGUE PARK

The Florida Marlins play the Montreal Expos on September 13, 2004, but they do not play in Miami or in Montreal. Because of the recent and impending hurricanes to hit Florida, the game is moved to a neutral, hurricane-free site—Cellular One Field, home of the Chicago White Sox. Over 4,000 fans are at the game—but fans of what is not clear. A percentage of the gate is donated for hurricane relief.

Off the field

"Baseball is like church. Many attend, but few understand."

Wes Westrum

A SAD AND MYSTERIOUS DAY FOR BASEBALL

"Big Ed" Delahanty, one of a record five brothers to play in the majors, dies when he falls, jumps, or is pushed from the International Bridge, a railroad bridge, in Bridgeburg, Ontario, on July 2, 1903. His body is found eight days later below Horseshoe Falls at Niagara Falls. Delahanty is elected to the Hall of Fame in 1945.

THEY WERE POETRY IN MOTION

"Casey At The Bat," by Ernest L. Thayer, first published in the *San Francisco Examiner* on June 3, 1888, is not only the most famous poem ever written about baseball, it's probably the most famous anything written about baseball. Coming in a close second is "Baseball's Sad Lexicon," about the Cubs' double play combination of Joe Tinker, Johnny Evers, and Francis Chance, by Franklin P. Adams, published on July 10, 1908, in the *New York Globe*.

These are the saddest of possible words,
Tinker-to-Evers-to-Chance.
Trio of bear cubs and fleeter than birds,
Tinker-to-Evers-to-Chance.
Ruthlessly pricking our gonfalon bubble,
Making a Giant hit into a double,
Words that are weighty with nothing but trouble.
Tinker-to-Evers-to-Chance.

A SAD DAY FOR BASEBALL
HARRY CLAY PULLIAM, PRESIDENT OF THE NATIONAL
LEAGUE, SHOOTS HIMSELF IN THE HEAD AT THE NEW
YORK ATHLETIC CLUB ON JULY 28, 1909, AND DIES
THE NEXT DAY. PULLIAM LEFT NO NOTE.

THE SALE OF THE "$100,000 INFIELD"
Connie Mack of the Philadelphia Athletics sells Eddie
Collins, another future Hall of Famer to the White
Sox, for $50,000 on December 8, 1914. The sale
starts the break up of the As' "$100,000" infield.

THAT'S NOT A BALL, IT'S A GRAPEFRUIT!
After boasting that he could catch a ball dropped
from an airplane, on March 13, 1915 future Hall of
Famer Wilbert Robinson prepares to catch the
ball. But a grapefruit is substituted. When it hits
"Uncle Robbie's" mitt, it explodes.

A TRUE BASEBALL HERO
Capt. Eddie Grant, a graduate of both Harvard
College and Harvard Law School, and a big leaguer
with the Indians, Phillies, Reds, and Giants, is killed
in the World War I Battle of the Argonne on October
5, 1918.

THE FIX IS IN
Conspiracies are joined and bribes are paid to members
of the Chicago White Sox between September 18 and
October 9, 1919 to fix the 1919 World Series.

THE CURSE OF THE BAMBINO

Short of cash, Boston Red Sox owner Harry Frazee sells his star pitcher and slugger George Herman "Babe" Ruth to the New York Yankees on January 3, 1920 for $125,000—an enormous sum at the time.

The Red Sox, who won the World Series in 1915, 1916, and 1918, would not win it again until 2004.

Ruth becomes the biggest star in the history of the game. He hits 714 home runs and leads the Yankees to four World Championships. In 1927 he hits 60 home runs, a record which stands as the single season mark until broken by Roger Maris—also of the Yankees—in 1961.

Can't do that any more

The American and National Leagues ban the spitball, the emeryball, the shineball, and all other doctored pitches on February 9, 1920. This is part of the game's effort to clean up not only the ball—which was frequently dirty—but also the game's image after the Black Sox scandal.

FIRST COMMISSIONER

UNITED STATES DISTRICT COURT JUDGE KENESAW MOUNTAIN LANDIS IS ELECTED THE FIRST "COMMISSIONER OF BASEBALL" ON NOVEMBER 12, 1920. HE SERVES UNTIL HIS DEATH IN 1944.

NOT GUILTY!
*A jury in Chicago acquits the eight "Black Sox"
players accused of throwing the World Series of
1919 on August 2, 1921.*

YOU ARE OUT!

Baseball Commissioner Landis ignores the fact that
eight members of the 1919 White Sox were acquitted
the previous day of fixing the World Series by a
Chicago jury. On August 3, 1921, he bans the eight
conspirators for life. The eight are: Chick Gandil,
"Shoeless" Joe Jackson, Swede Risberg, Buck
Weaver, Lefty Williams, Happy Felsch, Eddie Cicotte,
and Fred McMullin.

THE ONLY LEGAL MONOPOLY IN THE U.S.
*In a landmark ruling on May 29, 1922, the Supreme Court of
the United States declares that baseball is a sport and not a
business and is therefore exempt from anti-trust laws.*

RUTH MAKES $50,000 PER YEAR

In 1923, Babe Ruth of the Yankees becomes the first
player to earn $50,000 per year.

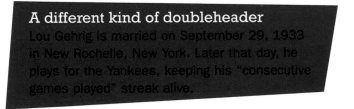

A different kind of doubleheader
Lou Gehrig is married on September 29, 1933
in New Rochelle, New York. Later that day, he
plays for the Yankees, keeping his "consecutive
games played" streak alive.

CA CHING!
Lou Gehrig will be paid $30,000 to play for the Yankees in 1935, a year after winning the triple crown.

COME FLY WITH ME
A new era in team travel is inaugurated on July 30, 1936, when the Boston Red Sox fly from Chicago to St. Louis—the first team to fly.

LOU GEHRIG DAY
July 4, 1939 is "Lou Gehrig Day" at Yankee Stadium. Felled by the mysterious disease Amyotrophic Lateral Sclerosis, later known as Lou Gehrig's disease, Gehrig bids farewell to baseball, and gives one of the most famous speeches in American history, proclaiming, despite his illness, "Today I consider myself the luckiest man on the face of the earth."

The Yankees bestow upon Gehrig a unique honor—his uniform #4 becomes the first number retired. Because Gehrig batted fourth in the batting order, when the Yankees originated uniform numbers, he was given #4. Gehrig is the only Yankee ever to wear #4.

CRYBABIES
A number of Cleveland Indians players sign a petition asking that management remove manager Oscar "Ossie" Vitt on June 13, 1940. The team earns the nickname "The Crybabies." Despite their protest, Vitt stays.

DEVASTATING
Cincinnati Reds catcher Willard Hershberger commits suicide on August 3, 1940, by slitting his own throat over a bathtub at the Copley Plaza hotel in Boston— the only major leaguer to commit suicide during the season.

SO LONG, CAPTAIN
LOU GEHRIG LOSES HIS FIGHT WITH AMYOTROPHIC LATERAL SCLEROSIS ON JUNE 2, 1941. HE IS 37.

BOB FELLER ENLISTS
Bob Feller enlists in the U.S. Navy on December 9, 1941, two days after Pearl Harbor is attacked. During his naval service, he misses four prime years of his career. He commands a gunnery crew on the Alabama and earns eight battle stars.

THE GREEN LIGHT LETTER
With the world at war, Commissioner Landis does not want baseball to seem unpatriotic by playing games while American soldiers and sailors were dying. So he writes to President Franklin D. Roosevelt, essentially putting all of baseball at the president's disposal. However, in what comes to be known as the "Green Light Letter," on January 15, 1942, President Roosevelt writes to Landis: "I honestly feel that it would be best for the country to keep baseball going. There will be fewer people unemployed and everybody will work longer

hours and harder than ever before. And that means that they ought to have a chance for recreation and for taking their minds off their work even more than before. Baseball provides a recreation which does not last over two hours or two hours and a half, and which can be got for very little cost. And I hope that night games can be extended because it gives an opportunity to the day shift to see a game occasionally."

A HAPPY COMMISSIONER
Albert B. "Happy" Chandler, former Governor of Kentucky and United States Senator, is elected the second commissioner of baseball on April 24, 1945. He is elected to the Hall of Fame in 1982.

> *ANOTHER BILL VEECK BRAINSTORM*
> *Indians fan Joe Earley got tired of the Indians holding celebratory days for various players and he asked the team why it never honored a fan. Over 60,000 fill the stadium in Cleveland for one of the goofiest promotions ever: "Good Old Joe Earley Night" on September 28, 1948. He is given some gag gifts, such as an outhouse, livestock, and a Model T Ford. Also a new convertible, kitchen appliances, and a watch.*

THE $100,000 OUTFIELDER
Joe DiMaggio of the Yankees becomes the first ballplayer to sign for a $100,000 annual contract on February 7, 1949.

If you can't be 'em, sue 'em

The United States Court of Appeals for the Second Circuit decides [Danny] Gardella vs. [Baseball Commissioner A.B. "Happy"] Chandler on February 9, 1949. Danny Gardella plays for the New York Giants in 1944, while the regulars are in military service. He then jumps to the Mexican League, where he doubles his salary. Baseball commissioner Chandler rules that any ballplayer who does not return to the big leagues by a deadline will become ineligible for five years. When the Mexican League collapses, Gardella tries to return to the big leagues in the U.S., but is blackballed because of Chandler's ruling. The only job he can find is as a hospital orderly. Gardella sues baseball claiming unlawful restraint of trade. He loses at trial, but wins in the Court of Appeals. Rather than appeal—and risk having the Supreme Court sustain the appellate court's decision— baseball settles with Gardella, and he has one at-bat for the Cardinals in 1950 before retiring. Gardella's case is a precursor to Curt Flood's 1970 lawsuit.

THE OLD PERFESSOR

Charles Dillon "Casey" Stengel makes his debut as manager of the New York Yankees on April 19, 1949. During his previous managerial career with the Brooklyn Dodgers and Boston Braves, his teams never finished higher than fifth place.

The Yankees win their first game under Stengel, and go on to win the World Series in 1949, 1950, 1951, 1952, and 1953—an unequalled five consecutive World Championships. Under Stengel's leadership, the Yankees also win the Series in 1956 and 1958.

SO LONG, MR. MACK. THANKS FOR 53 YEARS.

October 1, 1950 marks Connie Mack's final game as manager of the Philadelphia Athletics. (He also owns the team.) He retires after 53 years as a manager, with an incredible 7,755 games to his credit.

MARRIED AT HOME PLATE

Minor leaguer Don Zimmer and Jean Carol Bauerle are married at home plate in a minor league park in Elmira, New York, on August 16, 1951.

THAT'S A WRAP

Joe DiMaggio—The Yankee Clipper—announces his retirement on December 11, 1951. Although the Yankees offer him $125,000 to play another year, DiMaggio, knowing that his skills have diminished, says that there might be a fan at the park who has never seen him play before, and he doesn't want to play if he can't play at his best.

ON THE MOVE
The Boston Braves move to become the Milwaukee Braves for the 1953 season.

THIRD IN LINE
Ford C. Frick, president of the National League, is elected the third commissioner of baseball. September 20, 1951. He is elected to the Hall of Fame in 1970.

JOE AND MARILYN
Joe DiMaggio, the most famous ballplayer in America (even though he was retired), marries Marilyn Monroe, the most famous movie actress in America on January 14, 1954, at City Hall in San Francisco. The marriage lasts until October 10, 1955, when they are divorced. Many young male baseball fans know they are getting older when they realize that they are more interested in Mrs. DiMaggio than Mr. DiMaggio.

THE RED SCARE HITS BASEBALL

At the height of the McCarthy red scare, the Cincinnati team decides that its very name, "The Reds," is un-American. So, in 1954 it changes its name to "The Redlegs." They switch back to "Reds" in 1960.

GOING TO KANSAS CITY

Deciding that Philadelphia could no longer support two baseball teams, the Athletics move west to Kansas City, where they play their first game on April 12, 1955. They stay in Kansas City until 1967, when the move again, this time further west, to Oakland, California.

AT THE COPA

As New York columnist Leonard Lyons described it in "The Lyons Den:" "There are three great battlefields in American history: Gettysburg, Iwo Jima, and the Copacabana." On May 16, 1957, Yankees Yogi Berra, Mickey Mantle, Billy Martin, Hank Bauer, Elston Bauer, Whitey Ford, and Johnny Kucks and their wives are celebrating Martin's 29th birthday at the Copacabana, a well known New York City nightclub. Another patron shouts racial epithets at the performer, Sammy Davis Jr. A fight ensues. Lyons, familiar with the layout of the Copacabana, leads the Yankees out a secret exit. Berra's description is a classic: "Nobody did nothin' to nobody." Martin is traded to Kansas City on June 15. Ford, Bauer, Berra, Mantle, and Martin are fined $1,000 each.

SAY WHAT?

Casey Stengel testifies before a United States Senate subcommittee on July 8, 1958. The subcommittee is investigating baseball's anti-trust exemption. Stengel speaks for about an hour in his disjointed, rambling style known as "Stengelese." He had the Senators in stitches.

The next witness is Mickey Mantle. When asked his opinion of baseball's anti-trust exemption, Mantle replied, "My views are about the same as Casey's."

Ca ching!
Willie Mays of the Giants will be paid $90,000 for the 1962 season.

A THIRD MAJOR LEAGUE

New York City Mayor Robert Wagner announces plans for the Continental League on November 13, 1958, with William Shea as its chairman. The purpose of the league is to bring another major league team to New York City after the departure of the Giants and the Dodgers. Branch Rickey becomes president of the league on April 18, 1959. The league never gets off the ground, but the National League expands in 1962 to create the New York Mets. Their new stadium is named for Shea in 1964.

TRADE OF CHAMPIONS
1959 American League home run champion (42) Rocky Colavito of the Cleveland Indians is traded for 1959 batting champion (.353) Harvey Kuenn of the Detroit Tigers on April 17, 1960.

KABOOM!
The new scoreboard at Comiskey Park in Chicago is another Bill Veeck innovation. It explodes for the first time on May 1, 1960, when Al Smith of the White Sox homers off Jim Bunning.

Goodbye, Ty
Ty Cobb dies in Atlanta at the age of 74. July 17, 1961.

*IMPORTANT
Baseball Commissioner Ford C. Frick, a friend and ghostwriter for Babe Ruth, decrees on July 19, 1961, that if Babe Ruth's record of 60 home runs in 1927 is broken in the first 154 games of the season, it will be a new record. But if the record is broken after that, i.e., in the remaining six games of the new 162-game season, the new "record" will have an asterisk next to it

TRADE FROM HELL
The Cubs trade future Hall of Famer Lou Brock on June 15, 1964 to the St. Louis Cardinals for the one, the only, Ernie Broglio.

STILL NO EXPLANATION
For reasons never explained, on December 17, 1964, the Yankees fire Mel Allen, their long-time broadcaster, and one of the most popular people associated with baseball and the Yankees.

ABOVE THE FIELD
Lindsey Nelson broadcasts a Mets–Astros game from a gondola suspended 208 feet above second base in the Astrodome on April 28, 1965. Nelson became the first (and remains the only) person to broadcast a game from fair territory.

UNION! UNION! UNION!
Economist Marvin Miller is appointed Executive Director of the Major League Baseball Players Association on March 5, 1966. Under his leadership, the MLBPA becomes the most successful union in American history. At the time, the minimum salary in the major leagues is $6,000 per year. Arbitration, free agency, the end of the reserve clause, and the first collective bargaining agreement in professional sports become part of Miller's legacy. He will lead the MLBPA through 1983.

THE UNKNOWN SOLDIER

Lt. General William "Spike" Eckert (USAF, Ret.), who has not been to a ballgame in 10 years, is inexplicably elected as the fourth commissioner of baseball on November 17, 1965.

ONE OF THE WORST TRADES EVER

The Cincinnati Reds, having concluded that 1961 MVP Frank Robinson is "an old 30," trade him to the Baltimore Orioles on December 9, 1965, for Milt Pappas, Jack Baldschun, and Dick Simpson. Robinson is the American League MVP in 1966.

HOW TOM SEAVER BECAME A MET

When the Atlanta Braves lose their claim to Tom Seaver, $40,000 is all it takes to get him. Three teams put their names in a hat, and the New York Mets are picked in a lottery on April 2, 1966. Seaver becomes a Hall of Famer, and the greatest player in the team's history.

A MUST READ

The Glory of Their Times by Lawrence Ritter—one of the best baseball books ever written—is published in September, 1966. Ritter, a professor of finance at NYU, spent four years interviewing 22 ballplayers from the early part of the 20th century. Ritter splits the royalties with the players.

FAREWELL, DOUBLE X

Hall of Famer Jimmie Foxx chokes on a piece of meat and dies in Miami, Florida, at 59 on July 21, 1967.

SPIKED

Baseball commissioner William "Spike" Eckert resigns December 6, 1968, with three years remaining in his term.

BOWIE TAKES OVER

National League lawyer Bowie Kuhn is elected the fifth commissioner of baseball on February 14, 1969.

A FLOOD OF ISSUES

Curt Flood was an excellent outfielder for the St. Louis Cardinals for 14 years. He hit .293, won seven Gold Gloves, and was an All-Star three times. On October 7, 1969, the Cardinals trade him to the Philadelphia Phillies but he refuses to report. Rather than be traded without his consent, he sits out the season and brings an anti-trust suit against major league baseball challenging the "reserve clause" in Federal District Court (Flood v. Kuhn, 309 F.Supp 793, U.S.D.C., S.D. N.Y. 1970, Cooper, J.) He is ultimately sent to the Washington Senators on November 3, 1970. He loses the suit, and the Court of Appeals affirms the judgment, as does the United States Supreme Court on June 18, 1972. After 13 games with the Senators, Flood retires from baseball and moves to Denmark.

The Flood case paves the way for the end of the reserve clause, salary arbitration, free agency, and collective bargaining by players, even though Flood lost. Thousands of future players will benefit—just not Curt Flood.

BEST BOOK BY A PLAYER
Ball Four by Jim Bouton is published on June 1, 1970. It becomes the best-selling and most influential sports book ever written.

A BANNER DAY FOR BASEBALL RESEARCH
The Society for American Baseball Research (SABR) is founded in Cooperstown, New York, on August 10, 1971.

HE WAS BORN WHERE?
Future major leaguer Robin Jennings is born in Singapore on April 11, 1972.

HE MADE A DIFFERENCE
Jackie Robinson dies at 53 on October 24, 1972.

A true hero
Roberto Clemente, "The Great One," dies as his plane crashes into the sea off Puerto Rico, December 31, 1972. Clemente was bringing humanitarian aid to earthquake-torn Managua, Nicaragua. Clemente's career ends with exactly 3,000 hits.

WORST TRADE EVER
In the most notorious trade in baseball history, Yankees Fritz Peterson and Mike Kekich trade wives, children, and pets on March 5, 1973. Within a year, they are both with other teams.

FAREWELL TO THE LAST 19TH-CENTURY PLAYER
Ralph Darwin Miller, who played for the Brooklyn Bridegrooms in 1898 and the Baltimore Orioles in 1899, dies on May 8, 1973. The last survivor of 19th-century baseball was 100.

SURGERY WHICH CHANGED THE GAME
Dodgers pitcher Tommy John suffers a torn medial collateral ligament in his left arm. He undergoes ulnar collateral ligament reconstruction surgery, performed by Dr. Frank Jobe, in Los Angeles on September 25,

1974. During the procedure, a tendon is removed from John's right wrist and grafted to the elbow through holes drilled in the humerus and ulna bones. John returns to the game in 1976 and goes on to win 170 more games through age 46. Hundreds of players, mostly pitchers, later undergo the procedure, prolonging many careers. The surgery becomes universally known as "Tommy John surgery."

YANKEE OWNER SUSPENDED

New York Yankees' principal owner George M. Steinbrenner III is suspended for two years on November 27, 1974 because of his felony conviction for making illegal campaign contributions to the 1972 reelection campaign of Richard M. Nixon.

FREE AGENT SUPERSTAR

Peter Seitz, baseball's impartial arbitrator, declares Jim "Catfish" Hunter a free agent on December 15, 1974, setting off a bidding war for his services.

HOOKING A CATFISH

On New Years Eve 1974, Catfish Hunter signs a five-year, $3.75 million-dollar contract with the New York Yankees—the largest contract in history. His signing ushers in the era of big money free agents.

16TH GOLD GLOVE FOR BROOKS ROBINSON

In 1975, Brooks Robinson wins his record 16th Gold Glove for his outstanding glove work at third base for the Baltimore Orioles. (Jim Kaat also has 16 Gold Gloves.)

THE DAWN OF FREE AGENCY

Dave McNally and Andy Messersmith are declared free agents on December 23, 1975 when arbitrator Peter Seitz invalidates baseball's "reserve clause" which binds players to their teams in perpetuity.

A fabulous year

In 1975, Fred Lynn helps lead the Boston Red Sox to Game 7 of the World Series. He also does something which nobody has ever done before: with a .331 batting average, 21 homers, 7 triples, and 105 RBIs and 103 runs scored, he wins both the Rookie of the Year award and is named the Most Valuable Player in the American League.

KUHN VOIDS A GIGANTIC TRADE

Acting in what he calls "the best interest of baseball," commissioner Bowie Kuhn voids the Oakland As' proposed trades of Vida Blue to the Yankees, and Joe Rudi and Rollie Fingers to the Red Sox, June 18, 1976.

ANOTHER MUST READ FOR SERIOUS FANS

Bill James' self-published 1977 *Baseball Abstract* goes on sale in May, 1977. James establishes himself as the most respected, influential statistical analyst in the game. 30 years later, he still is.

A dreadful, spiteful trade

For months in early 1977, the talks between "The Franchise"—Tom Seaver of the New York Mets, who wanted to renegotiate his contract— and Mets management start at acrimonious and deteriorate from there. The city is shocked on June 15, 1977, when Seaver is traded to the Cincinnati Reds for four players. In 1983, he returns to the Mets. In his first start during his second stint with New York, the message board at Shea simply says "Starting Pitcher: #41." Seaver is inducted into the Hall of Fame in 1992.

WHAT'S THE SIGN?

Reggie Jackson of the Yankees ignores a sign in the tenth inning and tries to bunt on July 17, 1978. He pops up instead and the Yankees lose 9–7 to the Royals. Manager Billy Martin suspends Jackson for five days. Five days later, Martin explains his relationship with Jackson and Yankees owner George Steinbrenner: "The two deserve each other. One's a born liar; the other's convicted." Martin resigns as manager, to be succeeded by Hall of Famer Bob Lemon, who leads the Yankees to the World Championship.

MOST POPULAR PLAYER WHO NEVER PLAYED
Chico Escuela, as played by Garrett Morris, makes his debut—the first of ten appearances—on Saturday Night Live on November 11, 1978, when he speaks to the crowd at St. Mickey's Knights of Columbus. His most quoted line: "Baseball been berry berry good to me."

MILLION DOLLAR PLAYER
Nolan Ryan of the Houston Astros becomes the first ballplayer to earn $1,000,000 per season in 1979.

TRAGEDY STRIKES ANOTHER YANKEE CAPTAIN
YANKEE CAPTAIN THURMAN MUNSON, 32, IS KILLED ON AUGUST 2, 1979 WHILE PRACTICING LANDINGS IN HIS PRIVATE JET AT THE CANTON–AKRON AIRPORT NEAR HIS OHIO HOME.

POOF!
Billy Martin, the manager of the New York Yankees, is fired shortly after an October 24, 1979, barroom fight in Minneapolis with Joseph Cooper, a marshmallow salesman, who requires 15 stitches.

THE BIG "E" IN RED SOX LIGHTS UP

Fred Lynn (who in 1975 became the first player ever to be Rookie of the Year and Most Valuable Player in the same year) and Carlton Fisk become free agents when their team, the Boston Red Sox, mail them their new contracts two days late—one of the worst front-office blunders ever. The day is December 22, 1980.

Lynn, a Red Sox star from 1974–1980, winds up with the Angels. Fisk, a native New Englander and a future Hall of Famer, goes to the White Sox, for whom he plays more games than he played for the Red Sox.

HOW MUCH?!

George Foster of the Mets becomes the first player to earn $2,000,000 per season in 1982.

THE PETER PRINCIPLE

Travel agent Peter Ueberroth, who had helped the Los Angeles Olympic Organizing Committee turn a profit in 1984, is elected the sixth commissioner of baseball on March 3, 1984. He becomes commissioner on October 1, 1984.

A BAD OMEN?

The Expos trade Pete Rose to the Cincinnati Reds on August 16, 1984 for a player ominously named Tom Lawless.

JUST SAY NO!
Commissioner Peter Ueberroth disciplines 21 players, including Keith Hernandez, Joaquin Andujar, Jeffrey Leonard, Enos Cabell, Dale Berra, Lonnie Smith, and Dave Parker in connection with the worst drug scandal in the sport's history on February 28, 1986.

Renaissance man
A. Bartlett Giamatti, president of the National League, former president of Yale, and former professor of Renaissance literature and Romance languages, is elected seventh commissioner of baseball on September 8, 1988.

KIRBY HITS THE BIG TIME
Kirby Puckett of the Minnesota Twins becomes the first ballplayer to earn $3,000,000 per year in 1989.

A BRILLIANT DECISION BY GEORGE W. BUSH
George W. Bush, future president of the United States, makes what he says is the worst decision of his career. As chief operating officer of the Texas Rangers, he authorizes the trade of Sammy Sosa, Wilson Alvarez, and Scott Fletcher to the Chicago White Sox for Harold Baines and Fred Manrique on July 29, 1989.

You are out!
Baseball Commissioner A. Bartlett Giamatti announces at an August 24, 1989 press conference that Pete Rose has agreed to a lifetime ban from baseball.

> *TAKE TIME FOR PARADISE*
> *Baseball Commissioner A. Bartlett Giamatti dies in office of a heart attack at the age of 51 on September 1, 1989. He is succeeded by deputy commissioner, Fay Vincent, who is elected the eighth commissioner of baseball twelve days later.*

TRUE BASEBALL HERO
On July 6, 1991, major league umpire Steve Palermo is shot in the back in the parking lot of a Dallas restaurant after he heroically tried to help two women who were being robbed at gunpoint.

JACKPOT!
Ryne Sandberg of the 1992 Chicago Cubs becomes the first player to earn $7,000,000 per season in 1992.

SEVEN IS ENOUGH
YANKEES PITCHER STEVE HOWE IS BANNED FROM BASEBALL ON JUNE 24, 1992 AFTER SEVEN SUSPENSIONS RELATING TO NARCOTICS.

YOU CAN'T FIRE ME. I QUIT!

Fay Vincent resigns as commissioner of baseball four days after the owners vote to fire him by a vote of 18–9. He is succeeded by Brewers owner Allan "Bud" Selig, a former used car salesman from Milwaukee, as "acting commissioner" on September 10, 1992.

WATCH YOUR MOUTH

On February 3, 1993, Cincinnati Reds owner Marge Schott is suspended for a year and fined $25,000 for "racially and ethnically offensive" remarks, such as: "Hitler was good in the beginning, but he went too far," and for referring to a number of black players using a racial epithet. She is also ordered to partake in "multicultural training programs." The collector of Nazi memorabilia remains recalcitrant and unrepentant.

Spring training boating tragedy

Three Cleveland Indians pitchers are in a boat going an estimated 39 miles per hour when it crashes into a dock on Little Lake Nellie in Florida. Tim Crews and Steve Olin are killed. Bobby Ojeda is seriously injured, but returns to the mound later in the season, on March 22, 1993.

DEATH OF A PRINCE
Former major leaguer "Prince" Hal Schumacher
dies in Cooperstown, New York on April 21, 1993.

"THE GIANTS WIN HOME FIELD ADVANTAGE, THE GIANTS WIN HOME FIELD ADVANTAGE!"
Baseball owners decide on June 17, 1993, to expand
the playoffs from two teams in each league to four,
adding a third round of playoffs (the "Division
Series"), and also perpetrating on the game the
mediocrity-rewarding "wild card."

BIG EARNINGS!
Also in 1996, Albert Belle becomes the first
ballplayer to earn $11,000,000 per season.

A TRAGIC LOSS
*Umpire John McSherry dies of a heart attack
during the first inning of the Opening Day game
on April 1, 1996 in Cincinnati.*

THE KIRBY PUCKETT STORY
Kirby Puckett of the Minnesota Twins, one of the most
popular players in the game, wakes up with a black dot in
front of his left eye while in spring training in Ft. Myers,
Florida. He is diagnosed with glaucoma. Surgery does not
correct the problem, and on July 12, 1996, Puckett retires.
He is inducted into the Hall of Fame on August 5, 2001.

HONORING JACKIE

Nearly 50 years after his debut, Jackie Robinson's uniform #42 is retired throughout professional baseball on April 15, 1997. No new player, after this date, will wear #42. Those wearing it as of this date may continue to do so until they retire. The last major leaguer to wear #42 is Mariano Rivera of the New York Yankees.

A LEGEND PASSES ON
Joe DiMaggio dies at 84 on March 8, 1999.

WHAT—IF ANYTHING—WERE THEY THINKING?

56 members of the Major League Umpires Association resign on July 14, 1999, as part of the most misguided plan in the history of American labor. The aftermath of this disaster includes the decertification of the umpires union and the creation of the World Umpires Association.

STOP! WE HAVE A WINNER!

Alex Rodriguez, who has played for the Seattle Mariners for the first seven years of his career, signs a contract with the Texas Rangers on December 11, 2000. The contract will pay him $22.5 million dollars a year for 10 years, making Rodriguez the highest paid athlete in the world.

CAUGHT STEALING

The New York Yankees release outfielder Ruben Rivera on March 12, 2002, after they determined that he had stolen teammate Derek Jeter's baseball glove from his spring training locker and sold it to a memorabilia dealer for $2,500. The glove was returned to Jeter.

> ### BOY WONDER
> *Theo Epstein is hired to be the general manager of the Boston Red Sox on November 26, 2002. At 28, he is the youngest GM in history.*

BRAVO!

Arturo Moreno buys the Anaheim Angels on April 15, 2003. A fourth generation American of Mexican heritage, he is the first Latino owner of any major sport franchise, and the first member of any minority group to have a controlling interest in any major league baseball team.

YOU'RE IN!

On February 23, 2004, Al Clark, who, with 26 years of service had been one of the senior umpires in major league baseball, enters a plea of guilty in Federal Court in Newark, New Jersey, to conspiracy to commit mail fraud. Clark and his coconspirators had sold baseballs which they falsely claimed had been used in the 1978 Red Sox–Yankees "Bucky Dent" game; in

Dwight Gooden's no-hitter; in Nolan Ryan's 300th win game; and in Cal Ripken, Jr.'s record-tying and record-breaking games. At Clark's sentencing, Assistant United States Attorney Christopher J. Christie said: "There is something sacrosanct in this country about baseball and the special place in history some of its players hold. Mr. Clark knew that when he committed his fraud. Now a different umpire was making the call—and Mr. Clark has been called out on strikes." Clark was sentenced to four months in jail followed by four months of house arrest with electronic monitoring and ordered to make restitution of $40,000.

Lucky 13

The first game of a doubleheader between the visiting Yankees and the Philadelphia As on May 24, 1928 features 13 future Hall of Famers: the Yankees' Earle Combs, Leo Durocher, Lou Gehrig, Tony Lazzeri, Waite Hoyt, and Babe Ruth. The Yankee bench includes Stan Coveleski and manager Miller Huggins. The Athletics' Hall of Famers are Mickey Cochrane, Eddie Collins, Ty Cobb, Jimmie Foxx, Lefty Grove, Al Simmons, and Tris Speaker. The As manager is Connie Mack. The umpires are Tom Connolly and Bill McGowan.

Babe Ruth hits three home runs. For the only time in his career, he stands in as a righty—at least for two strikes. Then he strikes out lefty.

The Hall of Fame

"90% of baseball is half mental."

Yogi Berra

FIRST CLASS

Although they won't be inducted for three more years, the Baseball Writers Association of America votes for the first five members of the Hall of Fame: Ty Cobb, Babe Ruth, Honus Wagner, Christy Mathewson, and Walter Johnson, on February 2, 1936.

OPENING DAY

The National Baseball Hall of Fame and Museum opens on June 12, 1939, in the small (one traffic light) town of Cooperstown, New York.

TINKER, TO EVERS, TO CHANCE, TO COOPERSTOWN

Legendary double play combination Joe Tinker, Johnny Evers, and Frank Chance are inducted together into the Baseball Hall of Fame on June 13, 1946.

Honoring the men in blue

Thomas Connolly and Bill Klem become the first umpires inducted into the Hall of Fame on July 27, 1953.

THREE HALL OF FAMERS ON ONE PLAY

Ted Williams of the Boston Red Sox flies out to right fielder Al Kaline of the Detroit Tigers on July 20, 1958, and becomes the final victim of Jim Bunning's no-hitter. This is the only time that a Hall of Famer made the final out of a game by catching a ball hit by a Hall of Famer to end a no-hitter pitched by a Hall of Famer.

A great day for baseball

Jackie Robinson's election to the Baseball Hall of Fame makes him the first black man in the Hall. He is inducted on July 23, 1962.

BROTHERS-IN-LAW

19th-century stars Tim Keefe and John Montgomery Ward are inducted into the Baseball Hall of Fame at Cooperstown on July 27, 1964. They were married to sisters.

THE EYES HAVE IT

Chick Hafey is inducted into the Hall of Fame on August 9, 1971. He is the first Hall of Fame player who wore glasses.

BY ACCLAMATION

After waiving the usual five-year waiting period on March 20, 1973, the Baseball Writers Association of America votes to enshrine Roberto Clemente, who died on December 31, 1972, in the Hall of Fame.

YAWKEY WAY

Tom Yawkey, who owned the Boston Red Sox for 44 years, is inducted posthumously into the Hall of Fame—the first man so honored who was neither a player, a manager, nor a general manager, on August 3, 1980.

A FUTURE HALL OF FAMER GETS HIS 3,000TH HIT OFF ANOTHER FUTURE HALL OF FAMER
Dave Winfield of the Minnesota Twins singles off Dennis Eckersley of the Oakland As on September 16, 1993—Winfield's 3,000th hit.

PLAYERS INDEX